THE

GLASS

HOUSE

REVOLUTION

THE

GLASS

HOUSE

REVOLUTION

Inner-City War for Interdependence

LARRY ALAN BEAR

PUBLISHED FOR THE ACADEMY FOR EDUCATIONAL DEVELOPMENT
BY THE UNIVERSITY OF WASHINGTON PRESS / SEATTLE AND LONDON

Design by Wilsted & Taylor
Composition by Wilsted & Taylor

Library of Congress Cataloging-in-Publication Data

Bear, Larry Alan.
    The glass house revolution : inner-city war for interdependence /
Larry Alan Bear.
        p.   cm.
    Includes bibliographical references.
    ISBN 0-295-96929-6 (alk. paper). — ISBN 0-295-96930-X (pbk. :
alk. paper)
        1.   Inner cities—Pennsylvania—Philadelphia—Case studies.
2. Bell of Pennsylvania—Public relations—Case studies.
I. Academy for Educational Development. II. Title.
HN80.P5B43   1990
307.76'09748'11—dc20   89-24792
                                                               CIP

The paper used in this publication meets the minimum
requirements of American National Standard for Information
Sciences—Permanence of Paper for Printed Library Materials,
ANSI Z39.48-1984. ♾

This book is for my wife
Rita Maldonado-Bear
with love

CONTENTS

PREFACE

Late in 1986, I was contacted by New Era Philanthropy, a nonprofit organization engaged primarily in forwarding the philanthropic efforts of for-profit corporations on a rather broad scale. They had received an unusual request from Bell of Pennsylvania, one of the state telephone companies in the Bell Atlantic group. Bell of Pennsylvania wanted New Era to assist them in documenting the development of a specific project in North Philadelphia which Bell of Pennsylvania regarded as a first step toward the revitalization of that economically deprived inner-city area. Their hope was that the project might serve as an example of productive corporate citizenship that other large companies could choose to follow.

New Era's leadership felt that a book was called for, and when asked if I would be willing to undertake the task as their consultant, I was interested for two major reasons. As an adjunct professor of Finance at the Graduate Division of the Stern School of Business of New York University involved in issues of financial markets, ethics, law, and public policy, I was already at work on the subject of corporate social responsibility in general. Additionally, I had been interested and involved in overall community-development issues since the late 1960s, when I had served as New York City's Commissioner of Addiction Services.

In my initial meetings with both New Era Philanthropy and Bell of Pennsylvania, I tied my acceptance of the assignment to two major conditions. First, I would be given unrestricted access by Bell of Pennsylvania to all records, memos, papers, and files bearing on the project, as well as unrestricted access to all of the people in or out of Bell of Pennsylvania whom *I* felt were necessary to the proper telling of the story. Second, Bell of Pennsylvania would have *no* right of approval over the style, form, content, or conclusions of this book, either directly or through New Era; rather, all such matters would be within my sole discretion.

While Bell of Pennsylvania's legal department did insist (and properly so) on my signing a nondisclosure agreement regarding all Bell materials given to me but *not* used in this book, the final contract fully honors both of my conditions.

I have been given full and complete access to files and to individuals. Even more, I have been assisted nobly in arranging interviews and requesting materials by Bell of Pennsylvania people. Chuck Fulton and Denise Loughlin at Bell of Pennsylvania headquarters in Philadelphia must be singled out for help rendered above and beyond the call of duty in this regard.

The noninterference agreement has been honored absolutely. No attempt has ever been made to question my approach, my judgment, or my conclusions.

Nor has Bell ever tried to influence my pace of work, despite some impatience from time to time as my list of interviewees expanded well beyond what had been contemplated originally, and as my requests to the resourceful Chuck Fulton for ever more up-to-date information from his company seemed, to Bell, to be endless.

Each person interviewed and quoted in this book is identified by organization and title, and the date of the interview is cited. With one exception, all were interviewed in Philadelphia, Pennsylvania. That one exception was Bell Atlantic Vice President for Information Systems, John Gamba. Our meeting took place in Arlington, Virginia.

I want to acknowledge the editorial guidance of John Hochmann and the support of the Academy for Educational Development, especially Dr. Lee Hall, Senior Vice President and Director of the Division of Arts and Communications, for her belief in this project.

Finally, I must thank Jack Bennett, President of New Era Philanthropy, for his unwavering support of the entire project. His creativity, integrity, and friendship have always helped to assure rewarding growth experiences for me.

THE

GLASS

HOUSE

REVOLUTION

Philadelphia Computer Center. Lobby view from third floor. (Nona Short)

INTRODUCTION

Doers, undoers, and dreamers make up most of the real-life characters in this book: presidents, professors, corporate and academic types, a mayor, various officeholders, and inner-city people—some of them coming off very mean streets, challenging other people's peace of mind.

The story is all about building. Building ceilings and walls, surely, but equally important, building hope and trust and, ultimately, an extraordinary partnership aimed at inner-city regeneration.

The characters and their stories are inextricably linked to a remarkable physical structure. Long, but only four stories high, its outside is constructed of bronze-tinted glass. The inside, which contains some 225,000 square feet of space, is filled with equipment so smart and complex as to be beyond ordinary comprehension.

The large, tinted panels making up the building's outer skin allow light to shine in from outside, but they reflect to passersby nothing more than their own outdoors. The front entrance is slightly recessed, allowing a portion of the second floor itself to serve as a canopy over the earth-stone quarry tiles making up the plaza outside the main doors. Immediately inside, one finds lovely green plants, a soaring four-story atrium, and a high, curved desk complete with inquiring guard. Behind the guard are large, thickly glassed doors, keyed to a sophisticated card-access security system.

3

This building cost its owner relatively little to build in comparison to the cost of stuffing it full of the latest in silicon-based miracles: $25 million raised it; the bill for the state-of-the-art equipment inside will come to $100 million more.

The building itself is most unusual. For one thing, it contains two separate environmental control systems: one for the machinery, another for the people. Some of the equipment requires a warm, almost tropical environment, some a cool atmosphere. Continuous power monitoring stations control temperature, power surges, and other possible challenges to proper equipment functioning. Some floors in this building are raised two feet in order to accommodate mind-boggling amounts of electrical power feed lines, as well as the special piping needed to assure a constant supply of chilled water to machines whose generated internal heat might otherwise cause them to self-destruct. Moreover, there are special heat transfer systems which actively utilize permissible levels of equipment-generated heat as energy for warming the building itself. The building also contains under-floor water retention areas, special fire suppression systems, vapor barriers, fire stop cable vaults, special electrical power distribution centers, and two independent power feeds from the Philadelphia Electric Company, supplied through two separate substations and connected through an automatic switching system. If a transfer of current is made necessary by the failure of one substation, a battery-powered ride-through system (Uninterruptible Power System) will make the transfer of power undetectable to the excitable equipment. In addition, if *both* electric substations fail, the system will provide electric power for thirty minutes beyond the second failure.

Mechanical malfunctions inside here would present serious problems for the owner of the building, and for several million other people up and down America's Atlantic Coast who depend upon the ser-

vices performed by its phenomenal machines. Yet this edifice was built on a site sufficiently problematic to raise physical safety issues, and in the face of ferocious opposition from people whose own best interests helped dictate its chosen location in the first place. The building stands where it does because it was meant not only to produce the best in high-technology services, but to help as well in addressing one of the most crucial socioeconomic and political dilemmas currently facing the American people. Because of the importance of its functions and the broader implication of its existence, some discussion of what actually goes on inside this property is essential.

This building belongs to a telephone company: Bell of Pennsylvania. It is their Philadelphia Computer Center, and is more commonly referred to by Bell of Pennsylvania (and its sister organization, Diamond State Telephone of Delaware) as "the PCC."[1]

The tasks accomplished in the PCC do much to determine the quality and cost of telephone and other communications services in Pennsylvania and Delaware, and they relate as well to some services vital to the health and growth of other states and to our nation's capital.

The Bell of Pennsylvania PCC is, basically, a massive modern-age mechanizer. In view of its location, this makes the building itself a standing symbol for one of the great socioeconomic dilemmas of our time. But that is a subject for later discussion, and does not diminish the extraordinary nature of the work going on inside.

One might begin with the capacity of the PCC's key equipment.[2] There are five "mainframe" computers, which are operational twenty-four hours a day. While not "supercomputers," these mainframes are large machines which serve as the central processing units for the PCC's operations. Together, these large computers can perform hundreds of millions of calcula-

Philadelphia Computer Center. Some modern mechanizers at work. (Nona Short)

tions per second, and their individual storage capacity is awesome. In addition to their internal memories, these computers are linked to the PCC's direct-access storage devices, which is to say, to cassettes and the latest in disk technology, as well as to a large tape pool.

The total information storage capacity for all the equipment in the PCC is an incredible eleven hundred gigabytes. Since one gigabyte equals one billion bytes of information, that comes to a total of one trillion one hundred billion bytes (not symbolic bits, but rather language bytes) of stored and usable information. What this really means is that the PCC's equipment can store roughly the functional equivalent of the information contained in nine thousand complete *Encyclopædia Britannica*s.

These five mainframes are not the only operating computers in the PCC. There are also "minicomputers," referred to often as special-system computers, which do not relate to overall PCC tasks, but rather to particular applications. Most of these minicomputers rely for help on the mainframes, whose stored information encompasses many different programs and applications. They "talk" together in the course of performing tasks. In this respect, large mainframes, the central processing units, are referred to as "host" machines.

*Mini*computer is actually a confusing name, conjuring up equipment that might fit in one's pocket or pocketbook. In fact, minicomputer is only a comparative name for a computer smaller in size and with less capacity to store and deliver information than a mainframe. A mainframe is the size of a refrigerator; a minicomputer, though large enough, is almost always smaller. Mainframes sell for one million dollars and (way) up; minicomputers cost in the range of twenty thousand to one million dollars. Also measured in terms of size, memory, speed, and cost, the even smaller desktop machine is referred to as a

"*micro*computer," a real step below the mini. These more-or-less personal computers sit on just about every employee's desk in the PCC, at the ready to deal with some consequential piece of these eleven hundred billion available bytes of information.

What is actually accomplished with all this computer power?

A general response would be that the computers perform familiar functions in unfamiliar ways—functions that go to the heart of a telephone company's costs and services. The computers handle such matters as billing customers, dealing with service orders (i.e., installations and repairs), handling Yellow Pages advertising, processing inquiries and complaints, producing myriad reports, and allowing telephone company corporate customers access to Bell's computer capacities for their own use: for example, to generate their own financial data. This latter process is referred to as "time-sharing."

There are not only two major types of computers performing at the PCC (mainframes and minis), but two distinct processes as well. These are referred to as "real-time use" and "batching." Real-time use of information (also called teleprocessing) refers to those computer functions that are immediate. One simple instance might involve a customer and a service representative getting a job done quickly. When the customer phones in an order for a new type of service, for example, the Bell of Pennsylvania representative can take the information, determine the availability of both the materials and the installer, enter the order, and assign a delivery date to the customer—all in a very few minutes.

There are other excellent examples of real-time processes. The Business Office Support System/Billing And Collection System (BOSS/BAC) provides immediate on-line access to all customer records for six months back, for all Bell of Pennsylvania and Diamond State business offices. If called for, instantaneous record changes can be made: for example, by lowering a customer's bill. Some two thousand desktop computers scattered across two states can access data from the PCC mainframes and minis, and many desktop computers can already do this on multiple windows. "Multiple windows" refers to a computer screen's ability to hold up to four different pieces of data from PCC computer sources all at once. In this way, a business office employee could, for example, gain access to customer billing (the BOSS/BAC program), customer maintenance records (through a program system called LMOS), Bell equipment inventory records (referred to as TIRKS), and begin to process the customer's order (with a system called SOP/DOE) all together as part of the same real-time operation.

Real-time operations generally take place at the PCC between 7 A.M. and 7 P.M., although real time is approaching twenty-four hours a day with certain special police and hospital services. Batch time takes place from 7 P.M. to 7 A.M., so the PCC is actually a twenty-four-hour, seven-days-a-week operation. Batching refers to various tasks, done collectively, after the data to be used has been entered into the computer. For example, large amounts of data may be extracted from one system to update the information in a related system during batching time. One software program may tell PCC management in its fashion: "Here is interface information. You should extract from TIRKS and enter into ISOE (an improved service order entry system) the following data. . . ." Generating reports from various data sources is also a batch-time task.

There are some closely interrelated real time–batch time programs. A good example, and one which also illustrates the host computer–minicomputer interface, is COIN/CTOC. This program, fully spelled out, is the Coin-phone Operational and Information Network/Coin Telephone Operations Center Subsystem. COIN is the complete data base containing all coin-phone information for all 67,000 Bell-owned Pennsylvania and Delaware pay phones: where they are, what condition they are in, and even whether the coin boxes are full or empty. Statewide coin-telephone condition reports could be generated out of COIN during batch time. CTOC, on the other hand, is a specific microcomputer system software program that provides real-time access to data in COIN. It could determine, for example, *where* the full boxes are so that they can be emptied *now*.

The empty-it-now function is a simple example of how mechanization saves time and money. The COIN/CTOC combination replaces scheduled service calls that had to be made regularly, whether there was work to be done or not. Telephone company savings and productivity gains, accomplished by getting rid of tons of paper, service orders, microfiche, mountains of decentralized reports, and the elimination of time wasted between requests for assistance and actual responses, are certainly substantial.

This is the plus side of state-of-the-art computer equipment technology. The minus side is that expanding mechanization equals constricting roles and disappearing jobs for the equipment referred to collectively as "human beings." The PCC is clearly not a labor-intensive site. All of its twenty-four-hour-a-day multi-state operations, including administrative detail, can be handled by fewer than two hundred talented employees serving under a highly competent administrative leadership.

Computers, like human beings, of course, are not exempt from breakdowns. Monitoring the equipment in the PCC is a shared task: people and the machines themselves do it. The computers continuously use software (instructional programs) to analyze their own total operating environment. A machine reports itself in (on little screens, of course) to engineers. Some engineers are in the PCC, others are at a unique service center located off PCC premises. If a machine is giving notice that it could be turning temperamental, or even getting ready to die, the engineers determine when and why and put in motion preventive action—usually by issuing new computer commands. Screwdrivers, wrenches, and repairmen are definitely not de rigueur in our new computer age.

Meanwhile, the on-site PCC staff keeps hour-by-hour logs of real-time and batch-time availability. Ninety-nine percent is considered to be the *minimal* real-time performance standard for PCC computers. In fact, twenty-four-hour real time/batch time total system performance at the PCC has improved to approximately 99.9 percent.

Considering the massive amount of electronic information flowing into the PCC, and the equally voluminous amount flowing out, it is reasonable to ask: On what sort of transport vehicle does this information cargo ride? The answer, of course, is on "lines." There are lines in, lines out, and lines serving strictly internal PCC functions; some lines are multipurpose. Some idea of quantity might be had by examining a specific function: teleprocessing facilities in the Computer Communications Trouble and Analysis Center, inside the PCC, required five thousand pairs of cables at construction.

The "backbone" carrier network for the PCC "body" utilizes state-of-the-art technology to exploit the same two elements which determine computer capability: "holding capacity" (how many instructions a line can carry at a time) and "velocity" (how fast the instructions can be propelled from entry to exit).

Fiber-optic cable lines as thick as a human hair can carry brief bursts of electrical impulses (i.e., electronic bits and bytes of data) from many different sources at the same time, and at phenomenal speeds of up to several hundred million bits per second. The holding capacity of other kinds of cable lines can be boosted by the use of such equipment as multiplexors, which provide for the transmission of more than one message simultaneously on the same line (multiplex transmission). PCC multiplex lines easily deal with transmission speeds of 1.5 million bits per second from disparate sources. Its backbone network uses software program commands to switch data input and output from one line to another as well, thus cutting down on the total number of lines which might otherwise be needed to perform such a multitude of functions. The electronic, computerized, switching function is, overall, one of the most important components of all modern telephone service.

One example of PCC multiplex transmission, with switch-line usage, is its CYBER system. Bell of Pennsylvania/Diamond State corporate customers pay a fee to utilize the PCC's computer capability to input their own data and to have tasks such as financial analysis performed. They do this through the utilization of some two hundred lines connected to the PCC's special CYBER time-sharing computer.[3] The CYBER network handles some five hundred outside data "log-ins" (uses) each day.

The final element to be considered in this overview of the PCC is that of *security*. What I refer to here is not the security of computer content from theft or contamination. Every company must deal with those potential problems, whatever the nature of the business, and wherever they might be. Rather, what I refer to is the physical security of this building itself, all of its equipment, and its operations and personnel. Such security concerns, relative to the PCC, can be divided into two parts: the obvious and the extraordinary.

Obviously, enormous numbers of people and institutions rely on the PCC for uninterrupted services: 3.8 million Pennsylvania and Delaware residents and business customers, and, for certain functions, both the New Jersey and the Chesapeake and Potomac telephone companies as well (the latter serves Washington, D.C.).[4] The PCC's computers perform service order processing, customer billing, corporate accounting, on-line circuit installation and maintenance, record keeping, inventory control, in-house time sharing, and integrated force administration for and with other phone companies, together with a host of other functions, in the absence of which communications chaos could result along a major portion of the Atlantic Coast, including the nation's capital.

Certainly, Bell of Pennsylvania has not overlooked this security issue. A sophisticated card access system, a battery of closed-circuit TV cameras, and a manned security office on the premises of the PCC are evidence of that.

Nevertheless, there still exists the *extraordinary* character of this PCC's physical location. When plans for the creation of the PCC were under way, Bell Atlantic management manifested its anxiety about using a glass-covered building to house such sensitive equipment, data, and operations. And more than that, they were worried about using a glass-covered building in this specific Philadelphia area.[5]

Throughout 1984 and 1985, Bell of Pennsylvania had several sites available where it might have put up its PCC, both in Center City Philadelphia and in the surrounding suburbs. *Bell chose instead to locate its $125 million investment in the North Philadelphia ghetto.*

A nationally respected journalist, who recently traveled the nation at the request of the Ford Foundation to look at the phenomenon of Community Development Corporations, had this to say about the environs of Bell's PCC:

On our travels [my colleague and] I have visited ghettos and barrios across the United States. From Boston to Los Angeles to Chicago to Denver to Pittsburgh to Miami to Washington and Baltimore to New York City . . . let me tell you . . . we find North Philadelphia to be the grimmest ghetto in all of America. . . . Our photographer, who has seen deep poverty all over the world, described North Philadelphia as "our American Holocaust Museum." And not simply because of the poverty, but because there is virtually no other urban environment in America where the conscious neglect of the authorities seems so obvious.[6]

What is truly extraordinary about the Bell of Pennsylvania Computer Center, apart from its functions, is not just the decision to place it in North Philadelphia despite the initial concerns of its parent company, its board of directors, and most of its own employees. The staggering fact is that two successive chief executive officers of this billion-dollar corporation maintained their determination to have the PCC built in North Philadelphia well beyond the period of these initial concerns, and in the face of community rage and resistance, political harassment, and personal abuse.

There were times after the initial site location decision was made when even city officials anxious to have the PCC built in North Philadelphia couldn't understand why the location decision was not reversed. But, Bell hung in.

The point was reached where the telephone company's chief executive officer was forced to meet alone, face-to-face, after dark on lonely paths by Boathouse Row, with a powerful Philadelphia politician seemingly bent on his personal humiliation. But, he still chose to have Bell hang in.

Both Bell of Pennsylvania and its major partner, Temple University, made serious mistakes in the area of political and community relations, took setbacks, and paid dearly for them. Still, Bell hung in, determined to build in North Philadelphia.

Given the far more palatable personal and corporate alternatives available to Bell, the question of course is: Why?

Berks Street residence—still inhabited. (Lewis Downey)

What follows is the story of a strange partnership and struggle involving four dissimilar yet related communities—corporate, academic, political, and inner-city—and the people in each whose motives, strengths, and weaknesses brought about the "glass house": the North Philadelphia PCC. The story focuses on whether there truly is a way, within any major American city, to achieve technological excellence and corporate profit while *at the same time* promoting the economic and human growth of inner-city people. Because up to now such people have been abandoned, to the detriment of us all.

Philadelphia Computer Center interior. (Nona Short)

1

A PARTNERSHIP'S
BEGINNING

T he Bell of Pennsylvania Philadelphia Computer Center story begins
in 1982. In January of that year, a consent decree in
settlement of litigation was filed in a United States
Federal Court, to await a period of public comment
and negotiation with a judge. The parties to the decree were the Anti-Trust Division of the United States
Department of Justice and the American Telephone
and Telegraph Company. Ma Bell was about to move
out of the local telephone service business.[1]

In August 1982, the Court decree in the matter of
the *United States v. Western Electric and American
Telephone and Telegraph Company* was formally entered.[2] AT&T agreed to divest itself of all of its twenty-
two operating subsidiaries (including those of Penn-

sylvania and Delaware) and the United States agreed
that AT&T was to be free of all restrictions against their
competition in other than phone service areas. The
twenty-two former AT&T companies, which became
seven large regional companies, were prohibited from
favoring the old parent, AT&T/Western Electric/Bell
Labs, and would continue to be subjected to rate and
service regulations. In all other key aspects, however,
the children would be emancipated. The effective
hour set by the final decree was 12:01 A.M., January
1, 1984.

Bell of Pennsylvania, Diamond State, New Jersey
Bell, and the four Chesapeake and Potomac Tele-
phone Companies of Washington, D.C., Maryland,
Virginia, and West Virginia were brought under the

13

umbrella of one of the seven new regional companies, the Bell Atlantic Company, whose total assets today exceed $21 billion.[3] For Bell Atlantic and its constituent companies, 1984 would be their initial year of freedom.

That freedom should not be underrated. While AT&T had for years claimed publicly that its operating companies were allowed very broad managerial independence, the reality was different. The separate boards of directors of each of the twenty-two companies, for example, seemed to elect their presidents independently. In fact, the choices were predetermined at AT&T headquarters at 195 Broadway, New York City, and were overseen by AT&T officers holding seats on each regional company board.[4]

The newly granted communications independence of 1984 was not to be confined to Ma Bell's children. Many leaders in non-telephone company endeavors were quick to see that the coming market freedom in the telephone company business meant developmental freedom for them in the overall areas of computing and information systems. They might even be able, for example, to own and control some of their own lines and equipment.

One of these leaders was Peter Liacouras, the new president of Temple University in Philadelphia, whose institution later became a Bell of Pennsylvania partner. In May 1983, he appointed his special assistant, Robert G. Scanlon—presently Temple's vice president for Planning and Operations—to head a Computer Study Group. The charge: to develop a plan for a university-wide Computing and Information System with goals focusing on teaching and learning, research processes, administration services, the library system, and office automation and telecommunications.

The key goal was "to avail the University of the most significant cost-saving and technological opportunities *now available with the deregulation of the tele-communications industry.*" It was hardly coincidental that the final report of the committee was dated January 1984. The request for a proposal to construct such a system for Temple was now able, for the first time, to be circulated among many truly competitive bidders.[5]

Such competitive bidding at Temple threatened a possible future loss of business for Bell of Pennsylvania. From both a financial and a developmental point of view, however, the telephone company had more important problems. Its two computer centers in the Philadelphia area on January 1, 1984, had been transformed from children living free in their parents' house to tenants facing very high rents. In addition, if these centers, and the company itself, were to mature into state-of-the-art institutions, they had a lot of fast growing-up to do.

The independence offered both to the university and to the corporation set in motion forces which were to result in a unique partnership in the summer of 1984. This partnership would produce social and political upheaval in North Philadelphia in 1985, such as had not been experienced there in decades.

In January 1984, one of the two Bell of Pennsylvania Corporate Computer Centers (CCC) was close to its Philadelphia home office. The Schuylkill CCC[6] was located in the city on South 27th Street. The second center bore the name of the lovely suburban town on the Main Line in which it was located: the Wayne CCC.

Although there was no legal impediment to remaining as a tenant of AT&T, there were three good reasons why Bell of Pennsylvania management wanted to move out of those two computer centers. First, the buildings they were in continued to be AT&T property subsequent to the divestiture, and the rental charges to Bell of Pennsylvania would be about $4 million per year. Second, both centers together represented only 106,000 square feet of potentially usable space, and neither had room for the expansion necessary to accommodate future company needs, which were projected at closer to 200,000 square feet. The third reason was perhaps equally persuasive. After all those years spent under the corporate world's broadest wing, there was a strong yearning to get out and fly on one's own—to both feel and demonstrate independence. And what better way to strut one's stuff, to the advantage of both customers and shareholders, than to create one's own state-of-the-art computer center operation?

It was true that the seven Atlantic Coast local telephone companies were now under yet another big wing. But a brand-new Bell Atlantic was far less of a challenge to telephone company home rule than old Ma Bell had been. Bell Atlantic was a parent company younger than its own children, and new structures and processes had yet to be developed to deal with their mutual growth to maturity. In the meantime, local company responsibilities had to be met, and to do so properly demanded a high respect for local company rights.

No local telephone company of the old Bell System's total of twenty-two deserved more local autonomy consideration from a new parent than Bell of Pennsylvania. One of the oldest operating companies in the national system, dating back to 1879, it was also among the most technologically advanced.[7] In the mid-1970s it had eighteen electronic switching systems in operation in Philadelphia, more than existed in any other U.S. city;[8] it had also put into effect the first electronic billing system in the nation.[9] Given its technological development background and its existing leadership in Information Systems Operations, Bell of Pennsylvania in 1984 might have been expected to produce the plan it later did for a dazzling new computer technology plant.

Information Systems Operations (ISO) is a working division in Bell Atlantic and in each of the local

phone companies making up the network. ISO is at the heart of the telephone business, even though it never quite warms the hearts of company managers. ISO is responsible for developing new mechanical applications at both the subsidiary and parent levels and for maintaining essential functioning systems operations. Bell of Pennsylvania's ISO participated in the development, for example, of the fully computerized service order processing, direct-order entry system (SOP/DOE) which it is also charged with maintaining.[10]

For several reasons, ISOs, though certainly respected for their wizardry, are not embraced with warmth. ISO personnel are sometimes thought of as strange and not a little incomprehensible. In addition, they are often perceived as folks who are really carving a slice out of everybody else's pie. In that sense, ISO is a stepchild with no real in-house operation truly all its own. One can imagine business office personnel, for example, telling people at the PCC to "be careful there, you're dealing with *my* data!"

Then, too, ISO experts are prone to be hoisted on their own computerized petard. Everyone in the other divisions of the phone company who hears about a fabulous new product or process expects immediate personal possession: "If you were smart enough to get the data from four separate sources up onto the screen at once, why weren't you fast enough to get *my* multiple windows to *me* yesterday?"[11]

Finally, ISO must compete with paying customers for some of the resources it needs to do its job. Lines for transporting data are a good example. No matter that ISO's computer center lines help cut company costs and enhance productivity. Paying customers need lines, too, yet supplies and available installation hours do come up against finite limits. In addition, unlike paying customers, ISO people are expected to develop their own alternatives in the face of crisis. And so they do; hence the utilization of multiplexor data carriers which allows for more and more information flow in and out of the PCC on fewer and fewer lines.[12]

The head of the approximately nine-hundred-employee Bell of Pennsylvania ISO in 1984 and throughout the crucial period of PCC development and construction was Carl Kleckner, a communicative, personable man whose affable exterior never quite hides the tough, stubborn character inside. Like almost all the people who reach responsible executive levels in every U.S. telephone company, Kleckner has been a long-term Bell employee. His record was thirty-eight years with the local phone company, minus some time off to work with AT&T Central and Bell Labs, and one year as a Sloan Fellow at M.I.T. He was also involved with the development of Bell's Conshohocken, Pennsylvania, computerized billing system, the first such operation in America. So for Kleckner, reaching up to achieve 1980s state-of-the-art computerization was a natural progression.

Carl Kleckner and Bell of Pennsylvania's general objective, well before divestiture, had been to establish two central data centers for Pennsylvania, one in the eastern Philadelphia area and one in the western Pittsburgh area of the state.[13] There would be no need for any others.[14] The time for moving from general objectives to specific accomplishment was now. Kleckner and his personnel were ready, willing, and able. All that was needed was a decision, and direction, from above.

Seated above at divestiture time was Raymond W. Smith, a leader with a personality far more exciting than his family name. An engineering graduate of Carnegie-Mellon University, as well as the holder of an M.B.A. from the University of Pittsburgh, Smith is very good at dealing with mathematical and fiscal matters. He appears to be even better at dealing with human beings, which is rather more unusual for a finance man.

One reason for this is his ability to distinguish between real numbers and real people, a skill too often absent in economists and chief financial officers. "Numbers can be like ghosts," he claims. "They have the capability of being added one to the other. They can be quantified and manipulated. But they can never be trusted to represent such substantial human attributes as honor, dignity, commitment, and concern." The bottom line for corporate fiduciary Smith is not to be found in philosophy, but rather in profit and loss. Extensive reliance on "ghosts," like extensive reliance on administrative centralization, he feels, "eventually misses the human point [because] at a certain level you lose the human interplay, and low productivity results."[15]

Ray Smith, like so many other phone company officials, joined his state telephone company immediately upon graduation from college. He has served as Bell of Pennsylvania's vice president for Public Relations; general manager for the eastern region; vice president for Regulatory Affairs, and, for one year, director of Budget, Planning, and Analysis in the Office of the Comptroller at AT&T. Smith was named president and chief executive officer of Bell of Pennsylvania in 1983.

For Smith, who assumed the presidency in anticipation of the AT&T divestiture, there was never any real question about his company's need for developing and constructing its own master computer center. The puzzle was exactly where to put it. "A move to the suburbs *seemed* to fit the bill," but there were problems there.[16] Smith was personally committed to a corporate headquarters in Philadelphia. He felt that his company should help broaden the city's employment base, and that it should maintain a *public* posture of faith in the city's growth potential. Investing more than $100 million in a highly visible state-of-the-art computer center *outside* Philadelphia (and eventually closing down the center then in the city) wouldn't help at all.

The bottom line for President Smith was that Bell of Pennsylvania's economic health depended to a substantial degree on the economic health of the city; therefore, the act of moving its first independent major growth project outside would be indefensible from both the profit and the moral points of view.

Ray Smith's corporate leadership philosophy has one key element: there is no way, *in the long term*, to disassociate profits from morals. The corporate CEO, dedicated principally to the long-term best interests of his shareholders, can only further those best interests by conducting business in such a way as to promote the mutual growth of shareholders *together with* all others substantially linked in a positive way to the company's revenue-generating activities.

In today's economy, Smith's particular point of view is not so widely held. Actually, defining the nature and extent of *corporate social responsibility* and the corporate profit picture is an essential task for any true understanding of the PCC; however, that must come later. For now, it is sufficient to call attention to Smith's particular corporate leadership attitudes in order to relate them to a PCC in the ghetto. Smith's personal beliefs also helped bring him into a partnership with the mercurial man who had already cast his own organization's lot with the future of North Philadelphia: Temple University president, Peter Liacouras.

How you take to Peter James Liacouras would likely depend on your attitude toward constructive aggression. The product of six American universities, possessor of four earned degrees, attorney and international law specialist, former law professor, and law school dean, he took over the presidency of Temple in July 1982.[17] Hard driving, often abrasive, overtly political and ambitious, he nevertheless has not forgotten his humble Greek Orthodox family origins.

His inaugural address as university president contained two sincere and admiring references to his father, James, a man quite familiar with Aristotle despite his having had but one year of formal schooling. Both references by the son were to a philosophy of life that takes account of the need of all men and women to work hard and to strive for excellence, but above all, and very simply, to be both dependable and good.[18] Humanitarian and human rights awards from such groups as the National Convention of Women in Law and the American Jewish Committee of Philadelphia attest to son Liacouras's success in this regard.

The major decision Liacouras had to make upon assuming the Temple presidency was whether or not to move as many of the university's functions as possible away from its North Philadelphia main campus toward the suburbs. There are actually five Temple campuses: the Main Campus is centered at Montgomery and Broad streets in the heart of North Philadelphia; the Health Sciences Center, containing the University Hospital and the Medical/Dental School complex, is located not too far north on Broad; the Center City Campus is in the heart of Philadelphia; the Tyler School of Art is well to the north of the Health Sciences Center in Elkins Park, and, finally, the large, rambling Ambler Campus is located north of the Pennsylvania Turnpike in the quiet suburbs of Montgomery County.

Liacouras took over at a time when, largely because of its location, Temple was going through a twenty percent enrollment decline, a fiscal crisis, and an image problem in and out of the North Philadelphia community. The prior administration's response to all this had been to consider a gradual abandonment of North Philadelphia, with perhaps a steady, gradual movement onto the Ambler Campus.[19] The new president of this institution of higher education opted, as the new president of the local telephone

View toward Temple University from the Bell Philadelphia Computer Center. (Lewis Downey)

company would do several months later, to keep the business where his true headquarters was and to send the clear message to everyone in a position to be influenced by his decision that "despite whatever risks there might be, *we* are in North Philadelphia to stay."[20]

For Liacouras, some universities are meant to exist "as . . . proud island[s] separate from the towns and cities where they are found, but Temple isn't one of them," partly because Temple "is quintessentially a Philadelphia institution."[21] But mostly it is because Temple is a Philadelphia institution which aims not only to be one of the finest public comprehensive teaching and research universities in America, but, by virtue of its North Philadelphia anchor, to be a major educational agent for social change.[22]

The problem for Liacouras in 1984 was: how could Temple possibly go it alone? A private university dating from the 1890s, Temple had been made a state-related institution in 1965 by an act of the Pennsylvania legislature. However, while the state now covers some twenty-four percent of the annual university operating budget of approximately $435 million, the city of Philadelphia contributes less than one twenty-fifth of one percent, and that leaves a sizable sum to be handled in-house.[23] A sizable sum to have to come by in the face of the university's location, seen by many in the community as more of an albatross than an anchor. The community, apart from Temple, local churches, and a small core of hardy neighborhood activists, had been almost wholly given up for dead. Liacouras put it bluntly to Philadelphia's recently elected mayor, Wilson Goode, in 1984:

Our two [North Philadelphia] campuses can only continue the turn-around of the last two years, rather than a return to the earlier slide . . . if the campuses and the surrounding communities are strengthened. Otherwise, we will not be able to attract and retain a strong student body, faculty, and staff. . . . Benign neglect for a generation has permitted a pronounced deterioration of the North Broad Street strip. The losers have been the small businesses, surrounding neighborhoods, Temple University, and the City. . . . Rather than relocate . . . we have determined to stay . . . in North Philadelphia, [but] in the real world of university life, we cannot flourish . . . without a pronounced improvement in the quality of life in our neighborhoods, . . . without . . . vital small business [and] high tech businesses. . . . The abandoned houses and properties [problem] . . . must be corrected to improve our community. . . . The City, by whatever means possible, . . . should commit fully to . . . revitalization.[24]

The city of Philadelphia was willing to respond to Temple University's and North Philadelphia's needs to a greater extent than any previous administration, but it needed planning time and fiscal resources to do so. Plans could be developed, but the Philadelphia treasury had no funds.

Temple's own North Philadelphia commitment could not be confined solely to more minority students on campus. Out of its total student body of thirty thousand or so, it already had a 19.3 percent minority enrollment. This was as much as its sister state-related universities, Pitt and Penn State, combined.[25] Instead, Temple's commitment had to be to the *total* community in four distinct categories: the provision of health care, of education and research services, of community programs and activities of various kinds, and—basic to Temple and the community's very survival—a commitment to the revitalization of the economy of North Philadelphia.

While money would always be a problem, Temple did have the facilities to respond to the first three tasks. The fourth and last required a wholly new Temple concept, and Temple came up with it: a Science and Technology Campus and Jobs Program. But before such a concept could succeed, an immense initial act of faith, followed by an immediate commitment of money, had to be forthcoming from a source *outside* the university. Faith in, and dollars for, North Philadelphia required a far-sighted corporate CEO with a major company and a broad view of its social mission. The main ingredient this CEO would have to possess was a longer than three-month focus on his own, and his company's, bottom line.

President Liacouras and his director of Planning, historian James Hilty, went to work in 1982 with other top Temple personnel to structure a new main campus buildup. Ultimately, the non-academic steps taken to strengthen the image, presence, and core of the main campus were to better dormitory facilities, to move basketball activities and performing arts functions to the main campus, and to persuade alumnus Bill Cosby to get on TV with his Temple sweatshirt to let folks know how accomplished its graduates were—and just how well they could actually do.[26] Additionally, in 1984, Provost Barbara Lavin Brownstein began developing a comprehensive, long-range academic plan for Temple that would eventually involve the participation of hundreds of Temple faculty and staff. No single task, however, proved to be more immediately important to Temple's future than the plan for a master computing and information system assigned to Vice President Robert G. Scanlon.

Scanlon's report, as set forth earlier,[27] resulted in Temple's issuing a Request for a Proposal (RFP) for building the total system to several possible suppliers. Temple wanted bids from them describing and pricing the work necessary to achieve Temple's goal: a fully integrated voice, data, and communications product that would combine all computer, telephone, and video equipment needs, program designs, and processes into one basically fiber-optic, self-contained, university-wide telecommunications system.

The importance of the Request for a Proposal was not limited to the substance of the desired system. Temple included in the RFP a paragraph requesting each bidder to comment, beyond the design, construction, and maintenance of the system itself, on whether it would be willing to help Temple in the near future to forward its overall plans for development.[28] While not specific, and obviously not as important to Temple as the creative substance of the new system itself, and particularly its dollar cost to the university, the meaning of the paragraph was clear enough: your continued telecommunications presence, relating in *some* positive way to our ongoing development processes, will be of help to us in deciding which company will receive this contract.

Robert Scanlon was the chairman of the study group drawing up the Temple plan which served as the basis for the Request for a Proposal. Beginning his career as an elementary schoolteacher, Scanlon had progressed to the high post of Secretary of Education of the State of Pennsylvania by 1979. He had just completed his four-year stint in the state capital when he was asked by Liacouras in January 1983 to come to Temple to guide the university to a new focus on technological growth.

Temple, at the time, had some nine thousand phones on campus. The bottom-line question was whether it might not be more efficient for the university to have a new communications operation of its own. In light of the 1984 telephone company deregulation allowing for widespread competitive bidding, a cost-effective system could be designed specifically for the university. While Scanlon and his committee were working on this issue, Bruce Gordon at Bell of Pennsylvania was engaged in some work of his own.

Gordon, a native of New Jersey whose father was a high school principal and his mother a middle school teacher, was the highest ranking black executive at Bell of Pennsylvania. Now vice president—Special Assignment, in 1983 he was a marketing man. At that time, one of his efforts was aimed at persuading Temple to purchase a central exchange (Centrex) system for the university,[29] to be installed and maintained by Bell of Pennsylvania.[30]

Though they had one fundamental disagreement—whose telecommunications system Temple should have for the future—Gordon and Scanlon were otherwise quite compatible. For one thing, Gordon's father had been a professional friend of Scanlon's. Gordon and Scanlon shared some key perspectives on education. Moreover, neither was from the instant-gratification school; rather, they were devoted to long-term planning and to long-term business relationships.[31]

When the Temple Request for a Proposal was issued in January 1984, and it became clear that Temple would not remain as a fully dependent Bell of Pennsylvania customer, Gordon's attention turned to the areas that could be utilized to gain some continuing advantages for his company. For example, Bell could perhaps design the switches for the changeover and for the new system, do some rewiring and maintenance, and gain enough new knowledge overall to make itself a future marketer of similar new products. Mainly, what Gordon wanted was not to lose this large, longtime Philadelphia customer entirely, but rather to form a new, ongoing relationship of some kind. Such a relationship, he reasoned, would be in the best interests of Temple as well.

It was only natural that Bell of Pennsylvania should focus, too, on that paragraph in the Temple RFP which asked: apart from the brand-new system, what else might your corporation do for us down the line? Whatever might be done, Bell of Pennsylvania wouldn't have to travel very far to do it.

Bell Atlanticom, a Bell Atlantic Company telecommunications equipment division, became one of several major bidders for the new Temple system. Bell of Pennsylvania, while it could act as a subcontractor for Bell Atlantic, could not bid as the prime contractor on the Temple contract since it, unlike AT&T, was legally confined to those activities properly performed by a locally operating telephone service company.[32]

Bell Atlanticom quoted the lowest price of all the responsible bidders entered in the competition. Their winning bid was approximately $12.5 million.[33] Atlanticom also made it clear that they stood ready to act as Temple's helper in accordance with the general request in the RFP—and they had Bell of Pennsylvania to offer. Exactly what kind of help Temple might request, and exactly how Bell Atlanticom and Bell of Pennsylvania might respond, was not, of course, explicit. As yet, there was nothing to be explicit about.

Given the regional expertise Bell Atlantic's company was bringing aboard, the design and low cost of the bid, and the continuing close presence of a local telephone company familiar with Temple and in no geographical position to hide from responsibility, it is hardly surprising that Bell Atlanticom won the contract. The formal award was made in June 1984. It was now time for some discussion of what specific steps might be taken by Temple and Bell to further a long-term telecommunications-based partnership.

Clearly the time had also come for several personal agendas to coalesce. Bruce Gordon was a product of the turbulent sixties. Though he was socioeconomically a member of the middle class, he was also from Camden and familiar with inner-city realities. He had majored in sociology in college and was very much involved in the ongoing campus agitation for social change. Though he came late to thinking about being in business, it was natural enough that when he did, he should fasten on the notion of funding social change directly through the power structure—of using power, as Gordon himself puts it, "to aim corporate resources."[34]

As a highly intelligent businessman, Gordon recognized that if one was to help aim corporate resources at social concerns, one's first obligation was to see that these resources were consistently produced.[35] Every single person interviewed at Bell of Pennsylvania felt that his first two concerns were his responsibility to the public for the best telephone service, and to the stockholders for profitable operations. But all were also convinced that they and the corporation were obliged to consider the welfare of the communities in which they worked and prospered, and to take some sort of action to promote it.

Bell of Pennsylvania inherited the attitude that a telephone company must be socially responsible from its mother company.[36] Theodore Vail, president of AT&T from 1885 to 1889 and from 1907 to 1919, was a hard-nosed executive and a close associate of the robber barons of his day, yet in many ways he was well ahead of his time. While he shared J. P. Morgan's passion for monopoly, he did not share his passion for secrecy and for maximum profit at all costs. In his AT&T annual reports, he provided more information than any other executive of his time, stating in his report in 1911: "If we don't tell the truth about ourselves, somebody else will."[37] Vail came late to the notion that customers were as important as profit-sharing stockholders; however, that he came to it at all in the early twentieth century was extraordinary. Vail essentially decided that maximizing profit was not the *primary* objective of private enterprise. Profit had to be balanced with public obligations.[38] In 1910, while extolling the virtues of a telephone monopoly, he nevertheless said: "Society has never allowed that which is necessary to its existence to be controlled by private interests"; therefore, even his monopoly required regulation. Even more, it required regulation to the end

of "protecting the individual members of the public against corporate aggression and extortion." In sum, said Vail, the regulators had a "duty to restrain and suppress . . . certain evils that have been ingrained in our commercial practices."[39]

Actually, Vail was only the first in a line of Ma Bell leaders with interesting attitudes toward corporate social responsibility. President Walter Gifford told AT&T stockholders in a speech in 1927 to forget about extra dividends for "it would be contrary to sound policy for the management to earn speculative or large profits." The key to AT&T's success, for President Gifford, lay in his monopoly's "unusual obligation to the public"—not in unchecked individualism and short-term personal gain.[40]

Chester Barnard never made it to the top of AT&T, but he was vice president and general manager of Bell of Pennsylvania in the late twenties, and the president of New Jersey Bell from 1927 to 1948. A classical pianist, member of the American Philosophical Society, and later president of the Rockefeller Foundation, Barnard in the 1920s set up a program to send Bell of Pennsylvania executives to the University of Pennsylvania to study liberal arts, for the express purpose of broadening their horizons as corporate managers.[41]

Not all AT&T presidents were equally concerned about broadening personal horizons. Fred Kappel, who took office in 1956, used the word "liberal" as a pejorative. He is reported to have said, when faced with a speech writer's reference to an AT&T accomplishment in the past: "What do I care about history?" And later, when an aide attempted to make clear to him some of the nuances of a particular problem: "God damn it, I don't want to understand it, I just want to know what to do about it!"[42]

Not all AT&T leadership demonstrated intellectual openness and corporate social consciousness. Yet, given the enormous power they wielded, it is incredible that so many actually did. Hy Romnes, AT&T president from 1967 to 1972, was an engineer who tried hard to have his company relate to the tenor of the times. AT&T, he remarked in a public speech, had "to take account of complex social, economic, even political factors which do not figure in the contents of the Engineers Handbook."[43]

Of the historical Bell attitudes that came to the fore in Philadelphia in 1984, we focus finally on that of Cleo Craig, who ran AT&T from 1951 to 1956. A rigid fiscal conservative during whose term the AT&T debt-to-equity ratio dropped from forty-eight to thirty-three percent,[44] he never felt his company's net earnings were much more than barely adequate. With regard to corporate social policy, however, Craig went about as far out of the conservative mainstream as a chief executive could travel. His major effort aimed at removing from management all narrow, technician-type attitudes, and installing in their place a broader, more innovative approach. He hired a director of Management Development who is a story in himself: a politically conservative Quaker with radical management ideas named Robert Greenleaf. Craig referred to Greenleaf, who had direct access to him throughout his term, as his "kept revolutionary." Greenleaf revived Chester Barnard's humanities studies programs, taking twenty-one AT&T executives off the line and sending them to the University of Pennsylvania, with their families, for a full academic year. They were not to study management, but rather English literature, European history, Greek classics, and the like. During this year, the executives drew their full AT&T salaries. Craig's response to the University of Pennsylvania program was to inquire of Greenleaf why it was the only one AT&T sponsored. "We've got to get off our high horse," Craig told Greenleaf, "You aren't spending enough money."[45] Greenleaf thereupon set up similar, though shorter, programs at

Swarthmore, Northwestern, Williams, and Dartmouth.

Many at AT&T complained that such programs caused AT&T participants to become too "humanized" to act as corporate managers—complaints Bell of Pennsylvania felt then, and now, to be totally without merit.[46] It is interesting in this regard that throughout the mid-1980s, United States corporations were gobbling up liberal arts Ph.D.'s who, desiring to change direction and go into business, undertook special concentrated studies at select American graduate business schools. These "career in business" programs for liberal arts Ph.D.'s, pioneered by the New York University Graduate School of Business Administration, were commented on by Andrew Heiskell, a former chairman of the board of Time, Incorporated:

American business in general needs people who take the long view. It will rely increasingly on those who analyze the present based on an acquaintance with the past and a feel for the future, who consider the cost effective in light of the ethical, and who understand markets in the context of whole cultures.[47]

The Bell family was many years ahead of its time in this regard, but there is no evidence that any Bell System president ever forgot that he was running a business and not a social agency! Overall, the Bell System corporate culture has been more insistent than most in recognizing social responsibility.

There are three reasons for this sense of responsibility. First, Bell executives, by and large, have spent all, or almost all, of their professional lives in the Bell system. This attachment encourages, in addition to loyalty and commitment, a true feeling of belonging, of having a personal stake in the place. This translates in its broadest aspect to a true sense of, and appreciation for, *community*: theirs, the Bell community where they work, of course, but more: of belonging to and being responsible to the total community which you nourish and which also nourishes you. This attitude, this belief, is part of the Bell corporate culture and moves inexorably from the top down through the ranks.

Second, while every company benefits from the overall good health of the community in which it operates, most have the option to go to another one should the community sicken or die. Clearly, a local state telephone company has no other state, or area outside the United States, to which it can transfer its operations. It is therefore likely to have a clearer, more productive view of the community whose overall capacity to use its service will forever determine its bottom line.

Third, as cynics are quick to put forth, the Bell System had to keep everybody happy because it was regulated by public service commissions. This argument remains even after we point out that public service commissions have not always been strong advocates of the public interest, and that other regulated industries have not always demonstrated a level of social responsibility equal to that of Bell. However, if we do assume that the historical antecedents of the Bell System's culture of social responsibility are found in part in the regulatory function, that fact has little present significance. *How* one's social attitudes are formed is certainly not irrelevant; as far as people in the street are concerned, however, *what* those attitudes are is of much more practical importance.

Yet, if telephone company deregulation came tomorrow, would that event mark the end of the "community/social good" culture? Gilbert Wetzel, president and chief executive officer of Bell of Pennsylvania through 1988, responded to the issue this way:

There's no one in this business I've ever heard say that, thank God. Rather, there's an increasing awareness of people at all levels that it doesn't matter if you're regu- *lated or not. There's an intensely intertwined, complex society out there. No corporation can go it alone. To believe that is really foolish. Maybe the regulatory mind set has helped put us a quarter mile ahead of everybody else.*[48]

Even assuming a Bell System experience that helped put them ahead of everybody else, it still was not easy for Bell of Pennsylvania to make the initial decision to commit to a ghetto community perceived by everyone as somebody else's problem. It was not easy to maintain this commitment in the face of formidable protest and escalating costs. Nor was it easy to convince a board of directors that what was being done was, ultimately, an exercise in corporate responsibility to investors.

The PCC story is concerned with individuals and the judgments they made in individual circumstances. But their task, begun in 1984, can also serve as an illustration of the complexities, mistakes, struggles, and triumphs that characterize very special, *free market*, private sector, public sector, and higher educational alliances that are willing to harness the power of socially responsible corporate action to forward *both* profit and human progress in American inner cities. Such inner cities must be characterized, at present, as our nation's largest free market failure.

By July 1984, Bob Scanlon, Temple's top man in communications strategy, and Bruce Gordon, Bell of Pennsylvania's general manager for marketing and sales, were discussing what the two concerns could do for each other and for Philadelphia over the long term, and were carrying ideas back and forth to their respective power centers.[49] But another Bell of Pennsylvania officer with unique qualifications for seeing both Bell and Temple concerns very clearly was working even harder at this task than they were. He would become the key intermediary in this entire project.

Charles (Chuck) Schalch is a native Philadelphian who has served since 1983 as assistant vice president for External Affairs for Bell of Pennsylvania. Like so many other executives at every Bell operation around the country, his entire professional life has been spent with the telephone company. He came to Bell of Pennsylvania in 1958 after his graduation from college and three years as an army helicopter pilot, and progressed from local business office management to chief overseer of corporate contributions and economic development funding. Highly visible in Philadelphia, the quick-moving, quick-thinking Schalch, seemingly born to live with a telephone jammed into his ear, has enormous political savvy. He has also been involved with an astonishing number of the city's community and business organizations.

Yet, given his corporate persona and Bell of Pennsylvania loyalties, Schalch identifies not just with the telephone company. He is, far more than most, tied to Temple University, his alma mater. The university awarded him a business degree. Since that time, in his capacities as a university trustee and past president of the General Alumni Association, he has been presented with the alumni association's Certificate of Honor, the Distinguished Alumnus Award of the School of Business Administration, and the 1987 Distinguished Alumni Award from the university itself.

Schalch had been working with Jim Hilty, director of Planning for the new Liacouras administration at Temple, in the area of recruiting faculty and students. These two had certainly been giving some thought to how Bell and Temple might work out a new relationship as the university developed its new telecommunications system.[50] Both Gordon and Schalch had discussions together, and with their CEO, Ray Smith, and it did not take long for a pending Bell of Pennsylvania priority to be related to Temple. That priority involved Bell in making a de-

cision about how to proceed with a Bell computer center.

Quite independently of Temple, Bell of Pennsylvania had been dealing with its two major computer center concerns: the $4-million-per-year rents paid to AT&T for the Wayne and Schuylkill operations and the need to expand operations structurally and substantially in order to be state-of-the-art throughout the 1980s and beyond. Bell's Information Systems Operations division had prepared a needs assessment on this subject early in 1984.

The big questions were when and where—questions inextricably linked. The leading contender for a site was the Fort Washington Industrial Park, located in a small suburban area a few miles south of Temple's Ambler campus. Fort Washington presented the problem for CEO Smith of choosing to locate this substantial corporate investment, and operation, outside Philadelphia proper.

The location of the computer center real estate was, by July, a burning company issue. James Mackin, division manager of Real Estate for Bell, was drawn into the Bell-Temple partnership in the summer of 1984. A cynical, hard-nosed, yet incongruously talkative man, Mackin recalls being asked by CEO Smith in the early summer of 1984 to come up with "ideas, alternatives that Bell could work on together with Temple."[51] There did not seem to be any specificity to the request—certainly no reference to a computer center—and Mackin and his crew developed twenty-one ideas for cooperative ventures. It was not until the latter part of July that Mackin was asked to help develop a computer center plan, with the location on the Temple campus. Mackin assumed the site was to be Ambler.[52]

In July 1984, Gordon and Scanlon discussed Bell of Pennsylvania's problem with the one site Bell had been offered by developers near the Temple Ambler campus, in the Fort Washington Industrial Park.

One block east of the Philadelphia Computer Center. (Lewis Downey)

The building Bell would move into there required retrofitting, and Bell of Pennsylvania's ISO Division preferred a brand-new building instead. Bruce Gordon noted how close the Temple Ambler campus was to Fort Washington, that maybe something could be worked out in that regard, and was that not a creative idea?[53] Scanlon's response was, why not build your center on our central inner-city campus? Since no one at Bell of Pennsylvania had yet decided to *build* a center anywhere, not to mention in North Philadelphia, Scanlon's suggestion seemed very far out of everybody's vision—except Peter Liacouras's, of course.

Chuck Schalch, the perfect middleman, had put his CEO in touch with Temple planner Hilty.[54] As a committed alumnus, Schalch was aware of Temple's idea for an industrial park of some kind on its North Philadelphia campus. And as a Bell official Schalch was aware of his corporation's computer center dilemma. He had just helped to precipitate an examination of the possibility of tying Bell into Temple's suburban Ambler campus. Any *North Philadelphia* campus move, however, was beyond his jurisdiction. It was at this point, partly through Schalch's constant contacts and conversation with personnel from Bell and Temple, that Liacouras called Smith directly. The two presidents agreed to meet and tour Temple's North Philadelphia campus together as July drew to a close. For Ray Smith, at this point, the meeting was more or less a courtesy.[55] For Peter Liacouras, it was a good deal more.

Bell of Pennsylvania could perhaps turn out to be the initial partner Liacouras needed to reverse the process of commercial exodus from the North Philadelphia area, a partner who could actually help bring about social and economic change. If CEO Smith and Bell could be brought aboard, and then the city of Philadelphia, Temple might have a partnership that could help the city, the local community, and the

telephone company, while helping Temple to solidify its existence in North Philadelphia.

If he hoped to draw Smith into his vision, Liacouras knew he would have to open up to the Bell CEO. He would have to admit to all of his pressing problems and concerns, as well as his hopes for the future of Temple and North Philadelphia. There could be no holding back.

"Basically," Liacouras still feels, "it was a matter of trust—and I knew that he could dream."[56]

The physical area that Liacouras, Scanlon, Hilty, and others contemplated as the location for the Temple University Hi-Tech Industrial Park comprised 11.25 acres. It was situated at the eastern end of the North Philadelphia campus, and contained three enormous, Temple-owned commercial buildings in bad repair that were adjacent to railroad tracks formerly owned by the Reading Railroad. The largest of the empty Temple buildings, the Kardon Building, contained some 400,000 square feet of space. The other two, the Atlantic Terminal Warehouse and the Sjostrum Building, held some 100,000 and 172,000 square feet respectively.[57] Also situated within those 11.25 acres were some city property, a large parking lot referred to as Number 8, and, behind Number 8, an academic building. In August 1984, Parking Lot Number 8 showed up on maps as the furthermost southeastern boundary of the Temple main campus. The three buildings, with their more than 600,000 square feet of potentially usable space, together with a Temple physical plant and a steam plant building, really made up a separate group, a full block or so farther to the east of Parking Lot Number 8.

The Temple inner-city campus is not without its charms. It has some older Gothic buildings, tree-shaded walkways, new classrooms, dormitories, an impressive library facing a bell tower, a student union, and various graduate schools. But it is a small

View of the Kardon Building from the third floor of the Bell Philadelphia Computer Center. (Lewis Downey)

island in a far larger, less attractive inner-city sea: the poverty-stricken North Philadelphia area.

Standing on Montgomery Street, between 11th and 12th, facing Parking Lot Number 8, you have a city public school at your back, and to your left the bustling Temple campus. Off to your right, however, attractiveness fades fast. The three Temple commercial buildings can be described at best as gloomy, and the adjacent rail lines—with the South East Pennsylvania Transportation Authority's North Philadelphia train stop right there—as downright ugly. And that is in the daytime. At night, add danger to the atmosphere.

Even more sorrowful is what lies immediately beyond.

Adjacent to the university is what the Philadelphia Planning Commission refers to as the "Temple Area." Sixty-one percent of the households there are headed by a woman, approximately 30 percent of the labor force is unemployed, and over 50 percent of the population lives below the poverty line. Two-thirds of all the housing units are owned by people who don't live there. Over 81 percent of the population is black, more than 17 percent is Hispanic, and 40 percent are eighteen years old or younger. Still, things could be worse. And right next door, they are. Just south of the Temple Area is Ludlow, and adjacent to it, West Poplar. Ludlow has fewer female-headed households—only some 42 percent—but West Poplar counts more than 76 percent. In Ludlow, some 20 percent of the labor force is unemployed, but over 63 percent live below the poverty line. The ethnic composition of the neighborhood is approximately 49 percent black and 48 percent Hispanic. Not surprisingly, in Ludlow, less than 22 percent of the residents own the space in which they live. Still, in some ways, you'd be better off in Ludlow than over in West Poplar. There, a third of the working population can't find a job, almost 72 percent of the residents live below the poverty line,

and only 7 percent own any share of West Poplar's residential property. In West Poplar, some 92 percent of the residents are black and more than 5 percent are Hispanic. In West Poplar and in Ludlow the under-eighteen-year-old population exceeds 40 percent of the total residents.[58]

If ever kids were caught in a poverty trap, these surely are. And public education has never served them as a vehicle in which to travel the long road out. The percentage of persons in Temple Area, West Poplar, and Ludlow, twenty-five years of age or older, who have completed high school is 30.2 percent, 29.2 percent, and 23 percent, respectively[59]—an average no-high-school diploma rate of over 70 percent! The current crop of teenagers may better that figure, but not by an acceptable amount. Public schools in North Philadelphia today manifest the highest truancy, dropout, and absenteeism rates in the entire city system.[60] While the lack of a high school diploma doesn't necessarily translate into illiteracy, nor the possession of one into literacy, there is surely *some* correlation, and not solely with regard to intellectual growth, but even worse from the viewpoint of bread and butter—with regard to opportunities for employment.[61]

These then are some North Philadelphia ghetto statistics. The real horror is that they provoke no real horror in us at all. They are numbing numbers merely, a paper tragedy, beyond our capacity to feel, to comprehend, or to begin to deal with effectively. We don't seem to be able to grasp the reality of human waste as well as we do waste of other kinds. Chemical and radioactive waste, for example, *really* troubles a lot of humans. Perhaps that's because they see and feel the danger such offal poses to their personal health and the potential it has for turning their terrain into a wasteland.

Too many North Philadelphia kids and their families live, unhealthily, in an actual wasteland now.

Vacant lot near Philadelphia Computer Center, with fallen tree. (Lewis Downey)

Broad Street is the dividing line between the east and west sides of North Philadelphia. The Temple Area neighborhood and the university are east of Broad, as are many wasteland areas like Ludlow and West Poplar. Although the black population is substantial on the east side, it has decreased there over the last decade or so. It is even more concentrated now on the west side where in several neighborhoods it makes up close to 100 percent of the total. Hispanic numbers, however, are on the increase on the east side. There, in four of the nineteen neighborhoods, they make up 50 to 70 percent of all residents, and in three other neighborhoods, they make up 40 to 45 percent. The total North Philadelphia population, according to the 1980 census, was just under 280,000 people, less than 16 percent of whom were non-black and non-Hispanic. In 1930, the ethnic ratio was almost exactly reversed—whites made up 84 percent of the population.[62]

Girard Avenue, near the southern end of North Philadelphia, is a reasonable place to begin a tour of the area. It is quite close to the northernmost area of Center City, and it is a true example of inner-city non-cohesion. Girard Avenue serves as the southern or northern border for several neighborhoods, but instead of being the thoroughfare that unites them, it serves as a dividing line.

Both along and close to Girard, one can see typical examples of the strange North Philadelphia landscape. Here and there, as on little Marshall Street in the Puerto Rican community, there are some signs of life: fairly attractive smaller stores, shoppers, and cleanliness. But just around every corner is something falling apart—three-story rowhouses, for example, that are faded, decrepit, and looking for all the world like wooden dope fiends on the nod. The predominant feeling everywhere is emptiness—everything empty of hope, empty of warmth and sustenance, empty of real life. In fact,

much of the land and many homes do lie empty with nothing growing on, in, or around them, except for a maddening variety of decay. Vacant lots are especially terrifying, filled as they are with stinking bottles, rusted objects, noxious weeds, and parasitic vermin. Those are mainly what meets one's eye. Except, now and then, for a child or two, standing at the side of a half-deserted house next to one of those vacant lots, looking and waiting for God knows what—certainly nothing any youngster should be forced to find acceptable. One has to think about how many kinds of infections such boys and girls are subject to. And how outsiders could ever believe that they won't become contagious.[63]

At the corner of 7th and Girard, only the utterly innocent could fail to know that they were in the midst of a dope dealing center. Of course, nobody utterly innocent could survive in that vicinity. Ironically, a few blocks away from this corner, close to Girard and 5th, the North American Roman Catholic saint, Bishop John Neumann, lies buried in St. Peter's Church.

Many of the dwellings in these East Broad Street neighborhoods are the product of well-intentioned government "scattered-site" housing. "Scattered-site" refers to the policy of placing public housing in and around private housing rather than in separated enclaves. The idea is to integrate residences for the poor into the mainstream community. However, in such neighborhoods as West Poplar and Ludlow, there's nothing much left to integrate with, and a large part of the public housing stock is simply coming to pieces. Deterioration, abandonment, low income, low housing values, low or no credit availability—these are the elements that conspire to turn the hopeless and the helpless into *the* mainstream community.

Vacant lot east of Broad Street. (Lewis Downey)

It is ironic that the one development that might be thought of as actually giving North Philadelphia residents some hope has offered little but fear. It is not the kind of fear that comes in the night, with the dope dealers, the vandals, the muggers, and the randomly vicious; rather, it is the fear of not having a place to live at all: the fear of "gentrification."

As Center City residents earn more money, many also get the urge to move out—but not too far from where they earn, and where their social and cultural amenities are located. So they move a wee bit north and begin to invest in repairing and upgrading the outer neighborhoods. Most of the people already living in them are then caught in a double bind: they don't own the structures in which they reside, so they have no choice about the timing of the sale. And since they get no money when the real estate deal is made, they have no financial resources to bring with them anywhere else. So they haven't anywhere else to go.

Although the process of gentrification has reached more into the Spring Garden neighborhood area, west of Broad and on the very border of Center City, it is coming east now as well. Below Girard Avenue, in the Poplar Street area, a sizable amount of restoration is going on, particularly with the old twin houses that have always been known locally as "acey-deuceys." Until twenty or so years ago, these areas were not black or Hispanic, but were white immigrant.

In any event, the fear of gentrification, rather than the hope of neighborhood upgrading in which the locals participate, contribute, and benefit, was one force pitting some North Philadelphians against Bell of Pennsylvania and its $125 million PCC. We shall examine that force later in greater detail.

The western edge of the Ludlow area presses up close to the planned Temple Science and Technology Campus and the new Bell PCC. Just north of Ludlow is the Temple Area neighborhood, at whose southwest boundary sits the university's main campus.

Several parcels of real estate in the Temple Area are subject, technically, to the Temple Charette, a written agreement between Temple University and an angry community, signed on February 6, 1970. The Charette set up procedures for joint Temple-community planning with regard to the designated land.[64] Abutting the Temple campus are the Norris Homes, a public housing development of low- and high-rise buildings which have long been the subject of community concern.

Just beyond the northern edge of the Temple campus, near the old Reading Railroad tracks and heading west inside the Temple area, one encounters a sort of empty-ville. There are several hundred houses and lots there, of which a substantial number are in vile condition and vacant. Off to the east lies the Fairhill–West Kensington community/physical development area. Its five neighborhoods contain three of the five most heavily Hispanic populations in all of North Philadelphia. Here, too, is the same shocking North Philadelphia mixture of dissimilar blocks. Lehigh Avenue in the 7th Street area contains some nice looking public housing. Moreover, the area around 5th Street comprises the only Free Enterprise zone in North Philadelphia, and is the commercial center for North Philadelphia's Hispanic community.

Yet, close by this positive bustle lies the negative hustle of many Hispanic drug dealers who infect surrounding areas. In the vicinity of Orkny and Lawrence streets, and on a good deal of 6th Street, is the same sorry North Philadelphia signature: block after block of repulsive offal and crumbling houses, long deserted and deteriorating. Many of the streets lack identifying street signs—as if nobody really wanted to know exactly where in hell they were living.

After several blocks of this, the sudden sight of a tree is shocking. My final memory of this area is dope

Former crack house, cinderblocked. (Lewis Downey)

dealers passing by a sign reading: "Where Jesus Is First." At the very least, I thought, these jackals were running Him an uncomfortably close second.

West of Broad are many meritorious landmarks, such as the Nu-Tech Theater Entertainment Complex, the Martin Luther King Recreation Center, and the Wagner Institute. The Cecil B. Moore (formerly Columbia Avenue) development area, running from Broad Street west to 22nd, holds out some promise for both commercial and residential improvement; however, vacant houses and lots abound, quite close to some areas where housing is being renovated. Attractive public housing in some places sits on one side of a street, while on the other, crumbling walls look ready to fall under the weight of interminable despair.

The area west of Broad Street, overall, does seem to be in better shape than most neighborhoods in the east. One notices, for example, the presence of a good many parked cars in the west. Available data show that in the Temple Area, Ludlow, and West Poplar neighborhoods in the east, an average of 72 percent of all households have no automobiles available to them.[65]

The very bottom of North Philadelphia, geographically, is in fact, materially, the tops. Abutting Spring Garden Street in the south and the Philadelphia Museum of Art on the west, the neighborhood of Spring Garden West is a real example of material change. The area was blue-collar white some years ago, then Hispanic, and now, as Philadelphians put it, it's turned "Buppy" (Black Yuppie). Large, impressive apartment houses and new single and attractively refurbished rowhouses make up what is now a prosperous neighborhood on the very border of Center City Philadelphia.

The Puerto Ricans are moving north. An old sign, fastened on a pole at the end of a street not yet completely rehabilitated reads *No tire basura*, which means, Don't dump your garbage. In this neighborhood the sign itself now appears to be *basura*.

North Philadelphia is home to Temple University, and before leaving it, a comparison should be made with West Philadelphia, home to the University of Pennsylvania.

In West Philadelphia there is far less of each of the negatives infecting the north: very few destroyed buildings and vacant lots, and deteriorated and vandalized schools; less unemployment and fewer families living below the poverty line; less fear of personal and property crime; and fewer teenage pregnancies. There are more local jobs available as well, and people with the skills to work them.

The University of Pennsylvania, over the last twenty years or so, has become the West Philadelphia community. The area was never filled with the very poor who had to be pushed out. This is not to say that there were no local community people for the University of Pennsylvania to deal with, or that other community groups do not exist right now, or even that there are no poor people in West Philadelphia, because there are. But the base of the university community is a fairly well-integrated, liberal, educated population, settled into a geographical area more stable to begin with. And it has been the recipient of billions more in federal, state, city, and private funds for education, housing, and commercial investment in the last few decades than North Philadelphia ever saw. The University of Pennsylvania has already established a University City Science Center covering several city blocks on Market, one of the key streets in Center City. This Science Center is not the model for the one proposed by Temple, partly because the basic goals of the two projects are different.

A final comment should be made about the strengths rather than the weaknesses of North Philadelphia. There *are* local sources of development support and human sustenance, mainly certain black and Hispanic community coalition groups and, above all, churches with deep community ties upon whom the local people have always depended.

For example, the National Temple Baptist, whose nonprofit corporation is involved in participatory community housing renovation; the Zion Baptist, headed until very recently by the Reverend Leon Sullivan, the nationally respected developer of the Sullivan Principles related to United States corporate activity in South Africa; and the Bright Hope Baptist, headed by the Reverend William Gray, who preaches there every Sunday as his father did before him. As Congressman William Gray, he spends his working week in Washington, D.C., as a powerful and respected member of the House of Representatives. Both Gray's and Sullivan's churches have been sponsors of substantial public housing in North Philadelphia, while Zion Baptist's Opportunities Industrial Center has also done a good deal of job training. The Congreso de Latinos, ASPIRA, the Cecil B. Moore Business Association, and the East of Broad Community Development Corporation are but four of the many groups based principally *inside* the North Philadelphia area, which are working against difficult odds to forward economic and human development.

Not all local groups or churches are doing a creditable job of representing the best interests of local residents. To criticize those who are, however, on the basis that conditions are still very bad, is somewhat akin to lambasting the police in every urban area because crime remains a serious problem. If these spiritual and temporal community leaders who have been working so hard were to retire from the North Philadelphia battle, that battle would surely be lost.

The battle against the waste of human potential is one our country cannot afford to lose. As a nation committed to "freedom and justice for all," we are not honoring our moral obligation to fight this waste with

every possible resource at our command, and are suffering spiritually as a result. Additionally, because our nation exists in a vigorously competitive interdependent network of nations, such a loss of human resources is incompatible with national economic survival. At the very least, such a domestic waste of human beings is incompatible with the United States' survival as the major economic and socio-political power in the world.

Without knowing who said exactly what to whom, it is fair to state that when the presidents of Bell of Pennsylvania and Temple University met on the school's North Philadelphia campus in July 1984, the world power problem was not an item on their agenda.

But survival certainly was.

Peter Liacouras need not have been deeply concerned about Temple University's continued existence. But he would have been a fool not to have contemplated the possibility that the school for which he was now responsible could simply not continue to grow and prosper with its main campus located in a crumbling inner-city ghetto area. Even his detractors would fully agree that Liacouras was, and is, no fool. In July 1984, he had two seemingly incompatible realities to deal with. The first was his personal, and Temple's traditional, commitment to the populist tradition, the city, and to local community service.[66] Liacouras asked in his late 1982 inaugural address:

Can a university be fully satisfied about its health care, training, and research—when residents surrounding it grieve over an infant mortality rate higher than some developing countries? Can a university boast of its contributions to business and finance and the administration of justice, when virtually a third of the city's youth can find no productive work and see neither hope nor justice? Can a university which hosts

a 'Good Neighbor Day' for local youngsters each foot-
ball season be worthy of that name when these same
youngsters attend inadequate schools within the shad-
ows of our campuses? Can a university be complacent
when some people shun two of Temple's campuses be-
cause of fear?[67]

While Liacouras, more than most university presidents, understood both the nature of the community
problems surrounding his institution, and the mutual
hooks that bound them as long as they continued to
live together, he had this second reality to face. If
these hooks were to serve as upward rungs on a ladder,
rather than prongs for letting blood, North Philadelphia would have to be helped to achieve substantial
economic and social change. For this, he and his
abandoned community had to have a partner.

Ray Smith, too, had some interest in a partnership
in July 1984. The telephone company president was
conscious of his obligation, as a service provider with
a need for good customers,[68] and as a leader in the
Bell Atlantic family, to establish some new relationship with Temple. However, while Smith was prepared to explore possibilities, there is no doubt at all
that a commitment to ghetto revival was not yet
among them.

The Smith-Liacouras meeting lasted some two
hours.[69] During that time, they covered a lot of
ground, intellectually as well as with their feet. The
Temple president's pitch had to be straightforward
enough: we don't want to flee to the suburbs; we're
tied to the North Philadelphia community. "There's
surely no place I'd rather be."[70] We at Temple know
that what's good for North Philadelphia is good for us.
This community has to be revitalized. We've never
looked to attract businesses before, but that's part of
the answer. Specifically a new industrial park accom-
modating private companies which will forward economic development. And Bell can be the beginning.

Liacouras knew from Schalch and others that Bell
was ready to go forward on a new computer center,
and he offered Smith the Kardon Building.[71]

Smith took in both the talk and the surroundings.
The two men visited the Norris Homes low-rise housing, close by the campus on the border of what would
be Temple's Hi-Tech Industrial Park. The Bell CEO
was impressed with its "human size" and the possibilities that more commercial development could hold
for neighborhood regeneration. Still, Smith had several major concerns to resolve.

One concern had to have been the CEO's natural,
negative gut reaction to the abandoned, dilapidated
buildings and vacant lots, to the whole sorrowful experience of being on some of these mean streets. He
knew that they would be part of Bell's neighborhood
should the company buy in. Then, if Bell chose to
put a computer center in this Temple Area and nothing else followed, that choice could prove a disaster.
Smith could see no ultimate economic or social payoff from "a mere brave, symbolic gesture."[72] If Bell
were to make any investment here, it would also have
to make a commitment to some kind of meaningful,
ongoing participation in the revitalization of the entire area. Finally, the bottom line necessary for any
Bell investment would have to be the existence of a
solid, long-term, irrevocable Temple commitment of
effort and resources to their North Philadelphia
neighbors.

"Liacouras was really a tremendous advocate,"[73]
Smith feels. Liacouras was able to convince the Bell
CEO of his absolute and unshakable commitment of
resources to community growth, both as an individual and as the university's president. Interestingly
enough, Liacouras never tried to convince Smith that
he was thinking of Bell's best interests. His focus was
clearly on Temple.[74] This attitude made sense to a
CEO whose own focus was on the best interests of *his*
company and its investors. Behind the focus each

held, however, lay a more important, more basic, and shared belief, one based on the long-term view each felt was built into his leadership mandate: that company investment *aimed at improving the economic health of its actual or potential consumer base* would, in time, and if the product was a good one, improve the company's own long-term economic health—and its public image.

Smith and Liacouras seem to share another basic assumption as well: that a solid, lasting consumer base cannot be built on commercial investment alone. Economic development and human development have to go together. That assumption went very far, on a warm July day in North Philadelphia, in arguing for the creation of a special partnership between private industry and higher education.

Ray Smith left the Temple campus to return to his Bell of Pennsylvania headquarters building in Center City convinced of at least two things. First, that Bell of Pennsylvania could do well by doing good in North Philadelphia, if a proper time line and the involvement of all the necessary parties could be worked out. Second, that the Kardon Building was no place in which to establish a new corporate computer center.

The time line and the parties more or less went together—and long-term commitment was the key. Liacouras and Temple were in for the duration. But both Smith and the Temple president were in agreement that their two-sided partnership was incomplete; government participation was necessary. Smith wanted both state and city support over the long term. Curiously enough, as it turned out, it was in the very short term that state support became important.

Ray Smith's *immediate* concern, however, was not the state Capitol, or City Hall. The problem was his very own people.

When word went out that Bell of Pennsylvania was to have a new central, state-of-the-art computer center, and that the two existing centers would be phased out over time, few Bell employees were surprised and most were quite delighted; when word went out that the computer center would be close to a Temple campus so that Bell could benefit from the higher education resources available, such as faculty, research, and the like, and that Bell's employees could benefit from library facilities, student sports, social activities, and educational opportunities, many were surprised, but most were intrigued and quite positive overall. It would be nice, involved Bell employees generally felt, to be near the pleasant, suburban Temple Ambler campus.

When word went out that the main campus *in North Philadelphia* was the name of the game, management response ran the gamut from anger and resentment to despair and personal concern. The best response Smith might have gotten was bewilderment, and some at Bell were undoubtedly convinced that their boss's brilliance had gone over the wall.

Jim Mackin, Bell of Pennsylvania's division manager for Real Estate at the time, had been aware of the possibility of a computer center at Fort Washington, or close by, at Temple's Ambler campus. Still, he was amazed when he was informed in late summer that a center was in fact proposed to go up next to Temple and he was told to get a design team ready. He couldn't understand why Temple itself had decided to allow a commercial investment such as the Bell computer center to be placed in affluent Ambler. When Mackin was told later that the site was North Philadelphia, his reaction was that "people in this company just won't go up there." He was relieved to learn that the Bell commitment depended, in part, on city government cooperation. Mayor Goode, many thought at the time, "looked gubernatorial," and helping him and the city now would assure Bell's being thought well of in Harrisburg in the future. And if the city failed to help, "we could just walk away."[75]

Carl Kleckner, Bell's ISO chief in 1984, was ever the loyal warrior. He swallowed hard when he got the word. Prepared for the possibility of his baby being birthed at Ambler, his comment upon being told the center was going instead to Temple's main campus was: "Okay. Can do. But, boy, it's going to be troublesome."[76]

His top planner, Ed Parsons, worried about security.[77] So did a disappointed Harry Artz, his ISO district manager for Hardware/Software. Artz, concerned about the location of the "mechanized heart of the computer operation," would probably have been happier with the computer center hidden away in some suburban woods.[78]

The heaviest objections came from Bell employees in the Wayne computer center. They would be leaving an attractive, safe, Main Line suburban area to move into what they perceived as an inner-city battle zone. The bitter frosting on their already indigestible cake was the Philadelphia city income tax to which they would now be subjected.

As might be expected, there were those at Bell Atlantic and on the Bell of Pennsylvania board of directors who felt that this site location decision was, at the very least, questionable.[79] President Smith, therefore, had some selling to do at home, to his very own family.

There were some demonstrable pluses attached to the North Philadelphia computer center location. One was that the city electrical supply was superior, in terms of reliability, to any in the surrounding suburbs. Another was the company-wide agreed-upon importance of a serious Bell commitment to the headquarters city. A third was the center's location close to the heart of a major research university and its resources. In addition, the Bell executive leadership had attached some strings to the telephone company plan:

- *The city and state would have to work together with the federal government to relocate the Southeast Pennsylvania Transportation Authority (SEPTA) train station from its shabby, sometimes dangerous location, to one closer to the Bell building and the designated Temple Hi-Tech Industrial Park.*

- *The specific site to be built upon would have to be to Bell's liking and fit for its purpose in all respects.*

- *Temple had to find a second major business partner for its planned industrial park. Bell would not go it alone in this new development area.*

- *Temple had to commit itself to provide the Bell Computer Center with protected parking space.*

- *General area security would have to be provided by Temple University campus police.*

- *The city of Philadelphia would have to cooperate in several ways. Closing streets during construction time, and property transfers if necessary, were possible examples.*

Eleven such specified "requested commitments" are contained in an undated document in Bell of Pennsylvania files[80] whose contents establish two key facts: By mid-August 1984, Bell of Pennsylvania had reduced to writing rational ground rules for its commercial participation in the attempted rejuvenation of North Philadelphia. However, the ground rules put in writing for its community relations participation in the attempted rejuvenation were not rational at all.

Positive, productive community relations are crucial to the success of every major, highly visible, local corporate undertaking. Specific planning aimed at achieving such relations is essential, and this is most difficult with respect to communities composed mainly of the inner-city poor. Corporate planners in such cases need a specific sensitivity to the fact that poor people have a serious problem with trusting in the promise of productive and generous use of corporate and government resources for their benefit. This lack of confidence is firmly based on less than satisfactory past experience.

One of the "requested commitments" contained in the undated document already cited reads as follows:

[Bell of Pennsylvania requires] that all involvement with individuals or local residential organizations will be handled by [Temple] University or the City [of Philadelphia], and will be completed prior to the commitment of Bell of Pennsylvania's intent to occupy the area.[81]

Just what "involvement" the document refers to is an utter mystery. Certainly, any belief that attitudes and feelings about one's company on the part of thousands of disaffected citizens can be satisfactorily handled by others, even before one's company comes into the community, is, at best, unsophisticated. But when the main go-between is a university already perceived by the involved individuals and local residents as an unmitigated villain, that belief amounts to terminal naïveté.

Temple University insists—and not without some justification—that it has been, and is, the anchor for North Philadelphia. Temple is the area's largest employer, and is a generous supplier of medical, social, and educational services to many residents.[82] It has always had a communications problem, however, and tragically, it had a sorry record in the 1950s and 1960s of expansion and resident displacement.

The 1956 master plan for Temple University called for increasing the square footage of space that had existed at Temple in 1953 by four hundred percent. The school undertook expansion at a rapid pace. In its institutional development plan for 1966 it called for a campus four hundred percent larger by 1975 than that espoused in the 1956 plan. The Philadelphia City Council cooperated by changing the zoning status of some residential areas. By 1966, citizen petitions were circulating in the streets of North Philadelphia stating that "progress at the cost of human suffering is wrong."[83]

The Committee of Racial Equality in 1967 sponsored a new North Philadelphia organization called the Citizens Urban Renewal Exchange (CURE). In April of that year, CURE stated in a letter to the Temple University *News* that Temple and the universities of Pennsylvania and Drexel "have set their expansion programs on a collision course with the black communities in Philadelphia. This conflict has been brought on by the universities' insatiable greed for prominence, expansion, and utter disregard for the communities destroyed."[84] The heat was clearly on, but of the three schools criticized, only Temple was, geographically, in the kitchen.

In March 1969, a black student committee's rage was demonstrated in a list of demands presented to the Temple president: "The hopes and the aspirations of the black people surrounding Temple University have been blatantly injured in order to provide land for Temple's monstrously dehumanizing expansion." The committee went on to demand "the verbal and written assurance that Temple University has no intention of expanding any more . . . west or east of Broad Street . . . unless approved by the black community or its representatives in that vicinity unless provisions are made for the retaining of some black communities in the area of future expansion."[85]

Despite the obvious hyperbole and the fact that relations between urban communities and universities produced confrontation in many parts of the country in the sixties—for example, at Yale in New Haven and Columbia in New York—there was good cause in the North Philadelphia community for anger and concern. The result of the protests, after a series of Temple/community/city/state/federal government meetings, was the February 6, 1970, *Community-Temple Agreement of 1970*, referred to as "The Temple Charette." The *Agreement*, as signed by seven separate parties, sets out a figure of seven thousand people displaced as the result of Temple's expansion of its Broad and Montgomery Campus for over twenty years.[86] The bottom line of the *Agreement*, which defines certain land uses and sets up procedures for community consultation regarding certain land development, is that "society [should] pay . . . the higher cost of inner-city development rather than poor people through extensive loss of their homes."[87]

Peter Liacouras, at the time of these events, was a member of the faculty of the Temple Law School, where he progressed from assistant professor in 1963, to full professor in 1967 and, in 1972, to dean. During his time at the Law School, Liacouras established what seemed to be a very positive relationship with an ambitious young black law student named John Street. Street went on to become the councilman for the city of Philadelphia's 5th (North Philadelphia) district and, in 1985, the Bell/Temple project's bitterest—and most effective—enemy.

Although the actual land involved in the Bell of Pennsylvania project was not the object of specific restriction in the 1970 agreement, the overall issues of Temple land use, possible assessment hikes due to area development, and resultant displacement went with every single plot of ground. The political buzzword for all these concerns was *gentrification*. Bell of Pennsylvania's lack of attention to local history was a mistake for which they would later pay a heavy price.

Temple's current sociopolitical sensitivity, or lack of it, to the surrounding North Philadelphia community is a matter of some dispute. So is the accuracy of the community's perception of Temple as less than a true resource and friend to the neighborhood. What is beyond dispute is that Bell of Pennsylvania's initial dismissal of the inner-city community relations issue

as somebody else's responsibility was a truly grievous error. It is a bit puzzling that Bell should have made such an error in the first place.

To begin with, there was Bell of Pennsylvania's AT&T inheritance of a strong sense of community relations responsibility. And Bell of Pennsylvania's personal record demonstrated progress in this regard well beyond the parent's influence.

Most of Bell of Pennsylvania's high-level executives have spent substantial amounts of their professional time in areas related to the company's exercise of social responsibility. Ray Smith had served as the head of public affairs. When he pressed ahead with the PCC, Gil Wetzel, who replaced him as the president in 1985, was Bell of Pennsylvania's vice president for external affairs. Wetzel had risen to that vice presidency from the public affairs leadership position, one step below. And John Gamba, one of Wetzel's chief lieutenants during his PCC travails in 1984, later went on to become vice president for all Information Systems Operations at Bell Atlantic.[88]

Included in Smith and Wetzel's troops were thirteen Bell of Pennsylvania employees who served as paid full-time community relations managers throughout the state. Supervised by the district manager, these men and women are still involved in far more than simple public relations exercises. They help in the planning and execution of community programs ranging from health fairs and blood drives to neighbor days, tutoring, trade shows, and family nights. And of course, they dispense funds to local programs operating in the streets, in schools, and elsewhere. In all their endeavors, these specialists are aided by one or more of Bell's thirty-nine Community Relations Service Teams—Bell employees who volunteer to help evaluate local programs, needs, and requests in their geographical areas. It is clear that, beyond the millions of dollars given away as company donations each year, a good many of Bell's people continuously contribute their time, energy, and personal commitment to the communities throughout the state in which they work and live.

Why, then, this hurtful oversight in Philadelphia?

Perhaps one of the problems for Bell (and for almost every other large American corporation) is that relatively few corporate employees—and even fewer corporate executives—have ever worked and *lived* in an inner-city ghetto, or come from an economic and cultural background that would be conducive to truly understanding an inner-city neighborhood. Until recently, few large corporation employees or officers happened to be blacks or Hispanics who had worked their way up and out.

This is not to argue that a true sensitivity to the deprivations, aspirations, and anger of the inner-city poor can never be found among middle- and upper-class whites, or even that such sensitivities can always be found in black and Hispanic corporate employees. But sensitivity to the problem, like the existence of the problem itself, is mainly a matter of racial tolerance and concern. It would be hard to deny that intolerance and unconcern have a white face in America.

This general corporate inability to deal productively with inner-city communities, one would think, might also owe something to the fact that the poor usually don't make up any applicable portion of the paying corporate consumer base. It might, therefore, seem less important to become privy to their special concerns. There are exceptions, of course, in areas such as food, where government sponsorship provides the wherewithal by which the poor do become paying customers. But even here—as with a good deal of government-sponsored medical care—goods and services are delivered into an area of inelastic demand, quite often by persons and institutions who feel no need to be solicitous in terms of price or personal interest. Not surprisingly, the inner-city consumer response to the corporate provider is usually one of suspicion and distrust.

Community confrontation was on its way in North Philadelphia, but there were three major problems for Bell to resolve even before it actually arrived. The first was the negative in-house attitude toward a computer center shift to North Philadelphia. Of course, the depth of the resentment varied. The Schuylkill Computer Center at South 27th Street was already inside city boundaries, so for the employees there the migration was less difficult than for those in the computer center in suburban Wayne. There were concerned employees in Engineering, too, as well as in Real Estate, the non–computer center ISO, Public Relations, Economic Development, and other constituent portions of the External Affairs Division.

CEO Ray Smith's response was to take his case to his people. While he does not claim to have contacted every one of his company's twenty-five thousand employees, he certainly did speak face-to-face with most of them.

"I used my 'bully pulpit,'" Smith recalled, "to talk to groups of forty or more for up to two and a half hours at a time. And the issue wasn't just the PCC. It was company responsibility overall."[89] He wanted them to realize that their company had very large goals. "Not selfish, individual goals," but rather goals that recognized "the debt we, as a company, owe the public." Bell had to recognize that it and the people it served had joint interests, and that community service obligations arose out of that recognition.[90] Smith's final point to his employees: there is no conflict between community service, social responsibility, and corporate profits "in the long term. One hundred million dollars today [can produce] two hundred million dollars down the line, and all as the result of foresight."[91]

Smith was never really concerned about the capacity of Bell employees to appreciate and approve of the long-term perspective. He knew that his task was to take each person out of his own departmental tunnel view, so that he or she could begin to relate to the broader picture of corporate and public good.

Smith's companion and helper in almost all of the presentations was his vice president for External Affairs, Gil Wetzel. When Smith was promoted to vice chairman and chief financial officer of Bell Atlantic some six months later, and Wetzel assumed command, both executive and work force commitment to the North Philadelphia PCC decision was in place. Not everybody was delighted, but most were contacted, many were proud, and all were satisfied that they were at least important enough to have been kept informed by top management.

The second major problem for Bell to resolve had to do with the selection of a proper site. Temple officials were insistent that Bell rent its huge Kardon Building. At a meeting on August 29, 1984, Chuck Schalch, Jim Mackin, and then Bell Real Estate head Bob Young met with Temple's Robert Scanlon. Scanlon was told that Parking Lot Number 8 was what Bell wanted because it would place the computer center right at the main campus, which would be better for its employees, and not at the extreme east end. Moreover, Bell felt that the construction of a new building measured against alteration costs required for the Kardon Building would approximate a financial standoff. Not only would no extra cost be involved, but a new building erected specifically for a computer center operation would be easier and more economical to operate.

A disappointed Scanlon took the Bell representatives to see Liacouras, but he couldn't sell Kardon to them either. A possible rental price of two dollars a foot annually was mentioned. Bell found that interesting, but unrealistic. They suggested Temple review its total alteration cost estimates of three to five million dollars.

For Temple, Bell's move to the main campus was, in the end, more important than which site they finally occupied. Therefore, the conversation shifted to Bell's needs and concerns, assuming they purchased the Parking Lot Number 8 land making up the block between 11th and 12th Streets on Montgomery Avenue. The major problem for Temple would be to arrange for new parking space fast, since during construction, workers, building trailers, steel, bulldozers, and the like would occupy a lot of space.

Bell was assured of Temple's commitment to invest in renovations for the Kardon Box Factory Building, regardless of the Bell decision. Without extensive renovation, no major business would dream of moving in later on.

The final item at the August 29 meeting involved the community relations issue ostensibly dumped in Temple's lap. Liacouras assured the Bell people that "he would have the support of the Mayor, John Street, and [City Council president] Joe Coleman on this project."[92] Temple's president turned out to be two-thirds right about that. Unfortunately, for much too long a time, two-thirds wasn't half enough.

Although Bell did not intend to make a final, binding decision to build a new PCC at Temple until mid-October (the Fort Washington site remained as the alternative if things couldn't be worked out), Smith moved ahead "as if."[93]

Moving ahead meant facing up to the third major problem Bell wanted resolved: government participation in this initiative. Smith, Wetzel, and Schalch met, on separate occasions, with the executive director of then Governor Thornburgh's Cabinet Economic Development Committee in order to enlist state-level support for the PCC project; for example, for the provision of consultants and the possible creation of a Temple enterprise zone.[94]

Night scene east of Broad Street. (Lewis Downey)

Peter Liacouras also pressed for government support at the city of Philadelphia level. In a ten-page "Agenda Item" memorandum on October 8, 1984, addressed to Mayor Wilson Goode, with a covering letter stamped "Confidential," the Temple president summarized the details the two had covered six days earlier. Basically, Liacouras explained how important Temple was to North Philadelphia. He then described the plans for Temple's Hi-Tech Park and the need for city political and financial support, along the Broad Street corridor generally as well as in connection with the Park. Finally the memorandum focused on the key topic of their prior meeting:

By the 15th of October, a large high-tech company may decide whether or not to build a new 200,000 gross square feet computer center on Temple's existing Parking Area 8. . . . The choice is between Temple Town and a suburban location. The significance of this decision to all of us cannot be overstated.[95]

For Temple, using Bell as leverage for obtaining support from the city was not confined to Liacouras's pressure on the mayor. As early as August 31 when the Kardon Building was (in Temple's view) still a possibility, Scanlon had begun to seek cooperation from the executive director of the Philadelphia Industrial Development Corporation and the city's director of Commerce.[96]

Satisfied that proper government contacts were underway, that a satisfactory site existed, and that its employees had been properly prepared, Bell was ready to finalize its PCC decision. In October 1984, a formal memorandum was presented to Chief Executive Officer Smith which contained the following material:

Approval is requested to proceed with the detailed planning and engineering necessary to purchase land and construct a building at 11th Street and Montgo-

mery Avenue, Philadelphia, Pennsylvania, to be established as a consolidated Corporate Computer Center in the 1986 time frame. At that time, computer systems will be installed which will allow the future closing of the Corporate Computer Centers located in the Schuylkill and Wayne Buildings. This new center will serve as a replacement for all existing Liberty Region (Philadelphia and eastern Pennsylvania) Centers. The estimate of land and building capital expenditures required is $25.0 million. . . .

In a joint undertaking to revitalize a portion of our City, Temple University, and the City of Philadelphia, working in concert, have initiated plans to bring high-tech and more modern facilities into the northern section of the City. We can foresee a chance to contribute to this effort, while affording our Company the opportunity to further develop communication marketing strategies. A site is available for purchase in this area which will be conducive to the construction of a building for computer use, large enough to meet our needs for the foreseeable future and make a contribution to these revitalizing efforts and our corporation.

Therefore, your approval is requested to proceed with the detailed planning and engineering necessary to purchase [the] land and construct a building.

Under the typed word "Approved" in the lower left hand corner of the memo's final page is the signature "Ray Smith." The date is October 15, 1984.[97] The sale, purchase, and construction process had now begun.

The new computer center's problems had also begun. The first: Temple could not sell Parking Lot Number 8 to Bell. As it happened, they didn't own it.

Liacouras, Scanlon, and company naturally assumed that Temple Parking Lot Number 8 belonged to Temple University, but a memorandum in Bell's files set the truth of the matter out in a simple, straightforward manner:[98] the parcel of land turned out to be part of a State of Pennsylvania General Services Administration condemnation proceeding. Owned by the state, it was only leased to Temple. In order for Bell to buy it, an act of the legislature was necessary to authorize Temple to purchase it in the first place. The land had to get to Bell via Temple because of several existing complications, one of them being that it was located within a government designated Institutional Development District (IDD). This IDD would later become a kind of Temple-Bell petard on which the two huge institutions eventually could be hoisted by city councilman John Street.

The services of the late Alphonso Deal, North Philadelphia's representative in the state legislature, were enlisted to draw up the necessary legal approval for the sale, and the governor's office was notified. Fortunately, at the level of the State Capitol, the construction of Bell's new computer building on this particular site was properly seen in a positive light. The land transfer to Temple began moving along as quickly as anything might be expected to under a legislative roof.

Bell was fortunate that the land ownership problem at least was confined to one government entity only. The desired new Southeast Pennsylvania Transportation Authority commuter station stop demanded the cooperation of a public transportation authority, the city of Philadelphia, the State of Pennsylvania, and the U.S. Department of Transportation. In sum, a guaranteed catastrophe.

The need for the new commuter train stop was truly serious. The central subway station stop for Temple University, which is a rather nice one, is located at the corner of Columbia Avenue and Broad streets, four long blocks from Parking Lot Number 8, and more than six blocks from portions of the planned Science and Technology Park. During rush hours, that station is crowded; moreover, if one is a

non–city dweller, it is necessary to transfer from the commuter train system to the subway system and back, in order to use that stop each day, an uncomfortable and time-consuming process.

The local commuter train stop in North Philadelphia, only a block or so from the planned Park, was dirty, decrepit, and dangerous in the dark for many reasons.[99] Bell's original requirement that the existing SEPTA commuter stop be moved from Columbia Avenue between 9th and 10th Streets two blocks north to Berks was sensible, considered in terms of the comfort, convenience, and safety potential new Park tenants might be expected to require.

In 1984, the estimated planning and design costs of the new station, to be shared by Temple and the city, came to some $440,000. The actual construction of the station was to come to approximately $5,000,000 more, these costs to be shared by the federal government (75 percent), the city (8⅔ percent), and the state (16⅓ percent).[100] Mayor Goode pressed SEPTA to relocate the station. SEPTA completed a feasibility study, and memorandum and signatory paper preparers in each government system and subsystem began their inevitable chores. In December 1984, a Bell memo estimated three years till new station completion time. That was optimistic, since it is now 1989, and the old station is still in use.[101]

In December 1984, Temple appropriated $250,000, and the city $90,000 more, toward the planning and design costs for the new station, and they were joined by a third, most welcome, contributor.

Bell had demanded that a second major corporation for the contemplated Industrial Park move into a Temple-renovated Kardon Building before their own computer center went up. Temple, committed to the substantial costs of renovation, tried to find a co-anchor, such as the Mellon Bank, but was unable to locate another major business with Bell's particular motivation and long-term point of view. However, the Philadelphia Gas Works, a nonprofit quasi-public agency providing city gas, and already located in the general vicinity, was impressed with the Bell commitment. They informed Temple and Bell in late November 1984 that they were seriously considering constructing a new executive office building at Montgomery and 9th, immediately southwest of Temple's Kardon and Atlantic Terminal Buildings, and one-half block from the site of the Hi-Tech Park. PGW agreed to put up $100,000 to complete the funding necessary for the new station planning and design study.

As 1984 drew to a close, Chuck Schalch's role as Bell's coordinator for the North Philadelphia/Temple project was solidly established. On balance, it is clear that his joint connections at Temple and Bell served well to move this extraordinary partnership along. However, there were many people back then who manifested concern about whether Schalch might have to face some conflicting interests as time went on. And if he did, just how would he resolve them?

On December 19, 1983, Schalch represented Bell at a meeting with Temple personnel. There, in Liacouras's presence, he made it clear that the Bell project would not get under way without a co-anchor provided by Temple.[102] Eight days later, he wrote to his CEO that Bell must continue to insist on the SEPTA station change, the co-anchor, and the refurbishing by Temple of the Kardon Building. He stated further that he had insisted that Temple provide a project manager for "the entire Hi-Tech development process."[103]

Schalch very much wanted to help his alma mater and his city. Of that there can be no doubt. But Bell was the partner who brought him to the party and to whom he owed his primary loyalty. There is not one piece of paper in any file I examined, or any evidence presented at any of my forty-seven interviews, to indicate that Schalch ever acted contrary to that loyalty. Yet the man was sorely tested in 1985.

But then, so was everybody else, because it was in 1985 that tempers flared and battle lines were drawn by some public groups against bewildered corporate and academic people who believed they were embarked not only on an eventually profitable endeavor but also on a distinctly public-spirited one.

In 1985, the Philadelphia Urban Coalition, the Urban Affairs Partnership, the Institute for the Study of Civic Values, the East of Broad Street Coalition, Temple University, the mayor, the Department of Commerce, the city council, and Bell of Pennsylvania, among others, got down to business on an issue which, while focused on one proposed computer center in North Philadelphia, far transcended that singular operation. That issue goes by the name of "urban renewal."

The future of America's inner cities—and, by extension, the future of our nation—will be determined through the efforts which shape the focus and dimensions of urban renewal.[104]

Philadelphia Computer Center. Entrance seen from behind locked doors. (Nona Short)

2

COMPUTER
CENTER
AND
COMMUNITY

The Glass House War

For Bell of Pennsylvania, 1985 was to be the year of the Computer Center. A partnership had been created, focused on revitalizing Philadelphia's north-south axis, Broad Street. An eleven-acre, high-technology park was going to take shape in the heart of the Temple Main Campus. After years of watching the city's east-west axis develop—Penn's Landing, Society Hill, Market Street East and West, and the Penn-Drexel University Science Center—North Philadelphia was finally about to reverse its decline and begin to grow and prosper. The Bell of Pennsylvania PCC was to be the beginning.

Revitalization, however, would require going beyond erecting a building, to building trust and effect-ing cooperation through a broader partnership that fully included the community. That was a reality the Bell/Temple partners would very soon have to face.

Nevertheless, for Peter Liacouras, the Bell commitment was more than the fulfillment of a dream; it was the end of a nightmare. While the Temple president had had some support for the new technology park from the chairman of his board of trustees and a couple of others like Schalch, most of his trustees thought his commitment to, and his expansion plans for, North Philadelphia were "completely crazy."[1] So important was Bell's 1984–1985 corporate computer center location that in 1987, Liacouras could say, "If it weren't for Ray Smith, I don't think Temple would be where it is today."[2]

It was Smith's decision that Bell's stake in the future of its headquarters' city justified the investment in a reversal of the corporate exodus that, over a period of some two generations, had helped reduce North Philadelphia to an economic disaster area. But it took many more unusual people in addition to Ray Smith to give substance to this corporation–higher education–government partnership.

Bell ISO chief Kleckner's district staff manager for hardware/software, Harry Artz, chose one of those unusual people for the job of lead planner for the computer center. His name was Edward Parsons.

A thirty-one-year veteran of Bell of Pennsylvania, Ed Parsons' formal education had ceased when he graduated from high school. Yet his technical expertise and innovative design skills in the complex area of computers and computer support systems development were of such incredible proportions that his ISO fundamental plan for this $125-million operation was prepared with the help of six outside persons and an ISO staff of only three people![3] When pressed to explain how he could have managed to accomplish such a feat, the soft-spoken Parsons (who had refused a district head job in the past in order to remain online) reflected a bit, then said, "Well, don't forget, I'd been preparing for this job for thirty-one years."[4]

And he had. Parsons had designed the Wayne Center, had helped design the older Pittsburgh Center in the west, and had retrofitted the old AT&T building as a disaster backup for the Schuylkill Center.

This new North Philadelphia Computer Center, however, went far beyond anything Ed Parsons or anyone else in Bell had ever done. A computer model was built to project future growth for the PCC in order to determine Bell of Pennsylvania's technology needs for the next fifteen to twenty years.[5] This model demanded two levels of prognostication. The first required consideration of yearly historical computer growth increases and technology improvement rates by categories (central processing units and direct access storage devices would be two examples), to determine which state-of-the-art equipment would be required for the near future. The second required predictions of which equipment would be needed for the long term. Then space and support systems were to be designed for *all* of that equipment, *now*.[6] For example, mechanical and electrical system load requirements would need to be developed for all this miraculous machinery.[7]

"Imagine working with real estate people," Parsons said, "and saying to them 'Hey, we'll need to consider the following in very special ways: air, water, space, internal heat, cold, and all related areas—and for years to come.' Fantastic, huh?"[8]

Parsons's tiny group produced its completed fundamental plan for the new Bell PCC on May 26, 1985.[9] It covered eight areas of concern: costs, implementation strategy, large-scale application workload migration, teleprocessing network, assumptions, application testing strategy, personnel, and building. Of crucial importance was the process set up to migrate applications.

There was no problem making the decision to move only state-of-the-art *equipment* from Wayne and Schuylkill to the new PCC. The real planning concern was exactly how to move ongoing applications, or processes, from the two existing computer centers into the new PCC once it was completed. Some examples of such applications would be customer billing, service order modernization, coin telephone operational and informational processing, and time sharing.[10] While it would have been possible to replicate all of Bell's computerized applications anew, the cost of such replication would have exceeded the cost of migration by some 500 percent—and that cost would have been measured in the tens of millions of dollars.[11]

Even more involved was the planning for moving the networks over which the applications traveled to and from the existing centers. In some cases there were twenty thousand users per application out there, and all migrations would have to be effected without any ongoing computer service interruptions![12]

Beyond all technological planning, there was also the human element for Parsons and his team to deal with. People were also being moved and, in addition to their change of venue, there were concerns about changes in the way they were used to working. The district managers for Wayne and Schuylkill had a constant and not always contention-free input into some of the space planning decisions.

The one thing Ed Parsons could be certain of throughout the entire planning and construction process was the true nature of the computer center. Simply, it was to be a data processing factory which, if successful, would be a de-employment center. Bell's own projections showed that the personnel requirement at the PCC by the end of 1988 ought to total 195 employees, 13 *less* than the 208 at work in early 1985.[13] This fact in no way decreased the importance of the PCC building as a symbol of Bell's good faith to the nearby North Philadelphia community. However, as a straight one-for-one, accept-me-and-I'll-provide-jobs-for-you deal, it was bound to be misperceived, with resulting community dissatisfaction.

When he spoke to me, Parsons was very aware of, and concerned about, the broad socioeconomic and political implications attached to his company's newest structure.[14] He had often thought about the question of how mechanized his, or anyone else's, company should get. Jobs for people tend to disappear in proportion to the increase in state-of-the-art mechanization. His charge, however, was to have a computer center designed and built as well as it ever could be. The socioeconomic and political ramifications cre-

ated thereby were well beyond the hardware and software capacities he was dealing with.

Apart from the help Parsons received from his immediate superior, Harry Artz, and others in the ISO in planning and later executing the many application migrations, his closest colleague for the long gestation period in 1985 was Jim Mackin's designee in Bell of Pennsylvania Real Estate, Larry Momarella.

Momarella, who had come out of Penn State with an electrical engineering background, had started with Bell seventeen years earlier in Engineering Design and Management. He progressed into Real Estate, bringing to the PCC building design team an excellent interdepartmental fit. He and Parsons had done intensive planning work for a few months in 1984 on a new computer center without knowing where it would be. Parsons had by now moved physically into the Real Estate division with Momarella, and they were off and running.

By all the ordinary rules, this computer building should have taken three to four years to complete; however, it was scheduled to be finished in two.[15] This meant that it was going to have to be a fast-track job, one where one "package" or portion would be put out on bid while other portions were still being designed.[16]

Actually, Momarella and Parsons (the building's "owner" and "client," respectively) were the only Bell of Pennsylvania people on the full building design committee. The committee consisted of outside experts in architecture, structural design, and electrical and mechanical work. In addition, there was a construction manager and a computer room consultant. The consultant apparently had not had actual experience in designing computer rooms with areas as large as those envisioned here, but then, not many people anywhere ever had.

Momarella and Parsons worked long, grueling hours together, each of them enjoying very much

Berks Street at night. (Lewis Downey)

both the challenge and the company. Yet owner and client could, on occasion, find each other irksome. ISO's concern was structural and functional perfection, and Real Estate was not lacking in sympathy and understanding. They just happened to have a budget.

"ISO had a big wish list," Momarella remembered, smiling. "We leveled it sensibly."[17] Certainly the problems these two men dealt with interdepartmentally were never too difficult to resolve—even if, as Momarella's boss, Jim Mackin, felt, ISO people *were* "a little flaky."[18]

By March 1985 they were on track for a July 1985 construction start and a year-end completion. But balancing design and bidding schedules, however difficult, is one thing. Balancing and effectuating such schedules in the face of hostile community and political pressure, they soon learned, is quite another.

That pressure began building up early. On December 21, 1984, a lengthy article on current Pennsylvania executive branch activity appeared in the Philadelphia *Inquirer*.[19] It contained the following brief reference to a matter not even mentioned in the title heading of the published piece:

[The governor] also signed a bill authorizing the sale of state land to Temple University for the creation of an advanced technology industrial park at the North Philadelphia campus.[20]

A copy of the article, with that quote underlined and marked on either side of the column "??", made the rounds at a local North Philadelphia community activist organization called the North Central Unity Non-Profit Community Corporation. That group's files also contained other clippings with references to Templetown land, very early on in the high-tech park planning period: for example, "SEPTA plans to ask for corporate and institutional contributions to help pay for a new commuter train station near Temple University."[21]

Community members were quickly putting two plus one together and worrying about the answer. To them, the two were Temple University and government, the one was North Philadelphia land; the sum total came up: *gentrification*. All of which adds up to lesson number one for any private-public partnership aimed at undertaking development within an economically deprived community: never assume you can run so fast around the people inside that your project will zip by undiscovered. That is a dreadful way to go about building trust. Lesson number two: always be sure you understand from the outset the true focus of responsible community resistance.

Responsible community resistance is, of course, important to define. My own experience working in the area of inner-city community development[22] would indicate that when investments of any sort are proposed, three types of resisters tend to appear: the self-seekers, the nihilists, and those who are truly concerned.

The first group wants no more (or less) than a personal payoff, and can always be bribed by anyone foolish enough to make that destructive investment. The second wants permanent war in order to indulge permanent rage. Its members detest the very notion of compromise.

The third group holds the key to community development success. Because they are for the most part capitalists, like others outside their specific community, the people in this group are not averse to benefiting personally from outside investment. To denounce such benefits is to deny the validity of all the personally enriching activity undertaken by commercial and investment bankers, lawyers, doctors, CPAs, architects, and bishops—to name but a few major achievers in our general society. The bottom line, however, is that, as with admirable bankers, lawyers, doctors, CPAs, architects, bishops, and such, you can never pay truly concerned community people enough for them to betray the basic fiduciary relationship they feel they owe to the constituency of their community and its concerns and needs.

A serious partnership, dealing in good faith with a truly committed group about such primary concerns and needs, should find the experience, difficult as it might be, mutually growth-producing and rewarding. When dealing with such a group, compromise is not only permissible on both sides, it is generally essential. Even overzealous community residents who have every legitimate reason to feel betrayed and abandoned are remarkably willing to compromise with outsiders. They need to feel that these outsiders can be trusted to contribute positively, in a reasonable way and to a reasonable degree, to their community's development.

This third group within the community can and will deal with truth, even when it hurts. The inability, or unwillingness, to present truth openly to them is usually the investor's greatest problem. And this third group must be enlisted to help deal decisively with the purely self-seeking and the nihilistic groups.

These general observations appear to have been valid for Temple, Bell, the government, and the North Philadelphia community in 1985. In North Philadelphia at that time the main focus of responsible community resistance was gentrification.

The gentrification issue is much more than some special form of North Philadelphia community paranoia. Gentrification, as the term is used by inner-city residents today, refers to a process whereby their residential housing stock is upgraded, becomes high priced and highly taxed, too expensive for them to live in, and is soon occupied by upwardly mobile people, usually from a nearby center-city area.

Upgrading can result from initial direct residential property investment by owners, developers, and speculators, or by residential investment made subsequent to commercial property upgrading. In either case, since all but a very few ghetto dwellers are renters, not owners, they gain no benefit from property appreciation, only the loss of their living space. They also lose whatever sense of community they've managed to retain through a succession of lean, mean years.

Additionally, with gentrification, jobs for the poor tend to disappear along with the roofs over their heads. Even those small businesses, manufacturing and the like, that could have survived in the general economy are crowded out due to residence demand. Even if they aren't, there is still another problem: low-income workers forced out of the area may no longer be living within reach of whatever low-income jobs may be left.[23]

The gentrification problem is certainly not confined to North Philadelphia. It is of major concern in the District of Columbia, Chicago, New Orleans, San Francisco, and New York.[24] Recent articles have further detailed specific concerns in New York City's black Harlem and its Hispanic barrio, and a recent book has documented the problem in Hoboken, New Jersey, a basically blue-collar area quite unlike North Philadelphia's ghetto.[25] One writer has suggested that gentrification in America is "a concept that has come to seem so dull that many of us now classify it as one more insufferable cliche, one of the notions enveloped by its tedious buzzword (like the outrageously overused 'yuppie' or the now insipid 'urban blight' or 'renaissance')."[26] If this is true, then we are in a lot of trouble. Just as with the widening disparities in the division of wealth in America, the displacement and dismissal of the inner-city poor is not merely a matter of money. Gentrification has much to do with the kind of destructive class and racial divisions that weaken us as a nation, not only morally, but economically and competitively as well. In a newly independent, highly competitive world of far-flung countries, America, while seeking to maintain its international leadership role, can ill afford grave disadvantages originating right at home—disadvantages arising out of the poverty, alienation, pain, incapacity, and rage of those we have allowed in the midst of our plenty to feel like, and to be counted as, nothing.[27]

North Philadelphia's disaffected had a reasonable fear of being dispossessed by some upcoming action of Temple, but not because the university under President Liacouras was still unconcerned about the local residents being pushed out of the Temple area. To the contrary, Liacouras was aware of the gentrification problem. As early as October 1984, he had assured Mayor Goode, in writing, that community people living near the planned high-tech park would not be forced out. He wrote:

A major goal of the High Tech Industrial Park is to help improve the quality of life in the surrounding community. Under no circumstances should the residents of nearby public housing be adversely affected. . . . On the contrary, they can expect a positive impact from this development. . . . We envision no displacement of residents from this area, unlike the situations of the 1950s and 1960s.[28]

Moreover, there can be no doubt that Liacouras was personally sensitive to the problems and concerns of the communities contiguous to Temple, and determined to have his university play a positive role in constructive change. In his inauguration speech in October 1982, he said:

Temple must lead the way in developing real partnerships—not imposing our will but a real partnership—to revitalize our campuses, neighborhoods, and region. . . . It is intolerable to see injustice, incompetence, poverty, racism, and other prejudices choke off

the abilities and hopes of so many to the detriment of us all.[29]

Nevertheless, what was in Liacouras's head and heart was not clearly translated into such active Temple policy as North Philadelphians could see and trust. In the late winter and early spring of 1985, there were serious problems festering in the Temple area neighborhoods, particularly east of Broad Street, and they were understandable.

For one thing, painful past experience dies hard. The North Philadelphia area around Temple had gone through the Charette-related Temple displacement experience of the 1960s. And now, Temple was requesting help from the city not only for a new high-tech park, but also for development of an unused parcel of land for more parking space; for improved street lighting, security, and other services; for more space for Temple baseball, soccer, softball, and tennis fields; for a new indoor basketball arena; for a new track and field facility; and for a brand-new commuter train station.[30]

To most people, improved city services, new train stations, new commercial enterprises and close-by athletic fields and sports events mean a better quality of life for whoever lives in the vicinity. Temple's North Philadelphia neighbors would not have quarreled with that theoretical construct. Their problem was to determine *who*, in fact, would be living in such a vicinity. *They* never had, and based on all the real-world texts they'd ever read, it was not unreasonable to assume that they wouldn't be this time, either.

Community housing and commercial and recreational stock improvement do not have to equal displacement. The basic problem lies in the processes used in revitalizing an inner-city neighborhood in terms of housing, jobs, and services, *for the benefit of the people who live there.*

Processes focused on resident benefits have to be

long-term. Gentrification produces much needed municipal revenues in the short term. But local development for local benefit takes time. Even when community upgrading does come about, the taxing process must be carefully planned and higher taxes levied slowly. If not, local people will be hit too hard too soon; they will be forced out of neighborhoods by higher taxes levied on property they themselves have helped to improve.

Certainly, if municipal government has to forego some new sources of income in the short term, those who do pay taxes will have to ante up to support the long-term view. However, taxpayers are paying to sustain ghettos now, and gentrification only shifts, not solves, the ongoing plight of the taxpayer and the poor.

Here is one more example of America's ongoing struggle between the long- and the short-term view. Whether it is the merger, acquisition and arbitrage fast-payoff craze, our astronomical government, corporate, and personal debt, or the agony of the urban dispossessed which may be at issue, it should be clear by now that the short-term behavior and goals which have brought these conditions about cannot place our nation on the positive path to long-term good health and wealth.

It may well be argued that some balance is needed between revitalization of neighborhoods for the poor and the current housing needs of the middle class—in fact, that mixed neighborhoods, in some cases, could be one goal. However, there is no excuse for not focusing on alternatives to a neighborhood upgrading which is inevitably followed by displacement. For example, upgrading of the housing stock could be promoted through both public investment and local initiative and commitment, including provision for local home ownership and tenant housing management through "sweat equity" and the like, as well as through the use of public and private innovative

loans. Furthermore, zoning to protect small businesses from being crowded out by housing demand could also be considered.[31] One thing is certain, however: bitter conflict is likely to occur in the absence of a solid belief in the community that, however upgrading is brought about, residents will share in both costs *and* benefits.

"We've seen folks we knew kicked around in their neighborhoods before."

"Seven thousand shoved all the way out by Temple. Well the eighties aren't gonna be a repeat of the fifties and sixties."

Such comments were typical of what was being said angrily throughout North Philadelphia in early 1985, particularly in the neighborhoods east of Broad Street in the Temple area.

"You see, our major concern then," community activist Paula Brown Taylor says now, "was massive displacement. And we'd already gone through that."[32] The rallying cry was "no more." On the streets and in the churches a lot of people, for the very first time, were having their political consciousness raised by activists hard at work.

Paula Brown Taylor and Shirley Kitchen were two of these. Black women in their thirties, both had political experience as work organizers and committee persons in the 20th Ward of Philadelphia, where the main Temple campus is located. Aggressive, articulate, bright, and shrewd, both were familiar with the feeling of powerlessness that came from watching growth tear down, rather than build up, one's already weak social and economic base.

As part of their attempt to rally support for strong community resistance to what they saw as a secret deal between Temple and the city to dispossess them, they searched out possible allies. A key ally was Henry DeBernardo, a black local newspaperman and community organizer who also ran a neighborhood

Residential area east of Broad Street. (Lewis Downey)

youth development group called Aegis. Although he came from west of Broad Street, according to Paula Brown Taylor, "We had to join in one big effort to represent all of North Philadelphia."[33] DeBernardo would participate through the press in a fight against what was seen as a Temple plot, using Bell of Pennsylvania as a corporate wedge, to effect a thorough North Philadelphia gentrification.

If that initial reaction seems out of line with reality, this ought to be remembered: Paranoia tends to flourish in communities where experience has proven that no matter how poor you might be, you can still be stolen from. And you are more likely to be stolen from than you are to be given to by those who already have more than you do.

Unfortunately, Temple's most observable reaction to community anger was anger of its own, and this promoted further misunderstanding. Still, Bell was depending primarily on Temple to manage community concerns as its ISO and Real Estate divisions toiled on to produce plans for a fabulous computer center. Bell, Temple, and the mayor's office personnel, filled with the innocent happiness of those who expect to do well while doing good, prepared for a press conference announcing their laudable intentions. All the while, Henry DeBernardo was drawing up articles of war against them.

The first of his three-part series, "Inner City Squeeze: Battleground at Broad and Susquehanna," appeared in the Philadelphia *New Observer.*[34] Beginning with background on the community anger and resentment generated by the closing of the Elverson School in May 1983, later articles went on to cover, in DeBernardo's words, "vast, heretofore secret Temple University expansion plans, including the Bell computer center."[35] Hyperbole or not, there was no denying that the press conference to announce the Temple/Bell PCC, scheduled to take place on March 26, 1985, twelve days after the appearance of the first

DeBernardo piece, was going to go down badly with a lot of community people.

In the midst of preparations for the birth of its PCC, a major change occurred at Bell of Pennsylvania. Ray Smith was called upon by a shrewd and observant parent to serve as Bell Atlantic vice chairman and chief financial officer. Local Pennsylvania and Delaware telephone leadership devolved on Smith's successor on February 1, 1985.

The new president and CEO of Bell of Pennsylvania was Smith's closest professional associate, Gilbert H. Wetzel. A Penn State graduate, Wetzel, too, was professionally, fully Bell. As soon as he had completed a three-year hitch in the U.S. Air Force, he joined the company in 1958. He rose in 1982 from comptroller to vice president for public relations and external affairs, where he served until assuming the number one executive position. A rugged looking man in his early fifties, with a passing resemblance to the late American composer George Gershwin, Gil Wetzel at first sight projects strength, solidity, and endurance. Temple and the city would soon be drawing on these attributes to keep the North Philadelphia computer center dream alive.

The new president was not unfamiliar with PCC problems. When Smith had made the decision to deal head-on with internal company resistance, he had called on Gil Wetzel to help him carry the fight directly to employee meetings and talks, explaining the reasons for undertaking this project, and arguing vociferously for it.[36] By the time he took over as CEO, Wetzel's commitment to the North Philadelphia PCC was clear and unwavering.

At our interview, Wetzel said that "the focus for going this North Philadelphia route," was that "we knew we were big enough to make an impact on the entire Philadelphia business community." It was right, it was exciting, that Bell of Pennsylvania should be "the nucleus of economic development."[37]

"Think of how we felt," he said, grinning then with the recollection of past innocence, "when it turned out that people in the community actually didn't *like* us! We thought, why? We're here to help. What's wrong? What's going on?"[38]

What was going on was a formal buildup of community resistance. Paula Brown Taylor and Shirley Kitchen had progressed, in a very short time, from general organizers of resistance to leaders of a union of dissenters. They called their newly formed group the Save the Inner City Committee (SICC). And SICC was ready to bite.

Temple personnel were aware of the growing community discontent, but they made decisions that were not helpful in dealing with it. From the quite accurate point of view of Temple University's vice president for Administration, Patrick Swygert, and his office of Community Relations director, Tom Anderson, the university did have some community support for the high-tech center in general and the Bell computer center specifically.

Pat Swygert, a most competent educator and administrator and the highest ranking black executive at Temple, is an attorney who has served as General Counsel to the U.S. Civil Service Commission, and as a professor who still retains a position on the Temple Law School faculty. Politically experienced, he was convinced in 1985, and still is now, that what Temple had in 1985 was "community support"; and what the community dissenters had was "political opposition."[39]

Political it was, indeed, but successful community opposition always is—just as is successful community support. Vice President Swygert's integrity, intelligence, and absolute commitment to North Philadelphia's development, as well as to the overall minority struggle for a meaningful place in the economic

mainstream, are undeniable. It can surely be argued, however, that his community/politics distinction (between "us" and "them") was, and is, a distinction without much substance.

Major community support *for* the Bell-Temple project was led by the Reverend J. Jerome Cooper of the Berean Presbyterian Church and his North Central Philadelphia Association (NCPA). The NCPA was considered by many people in the area to be a "Temple front."[40] Whether allegations such as "Cooper and Temple Official Patrick Swygert have admitted to press sources that the NCPA is solely funded by Temple"[41] are accurate, either in the facts stated or in the conclusions supposed to be drawn therefrom, is not wholly the issue.

What is important, and certainly true as stated by the Reverend Cooper himself during the time of community conflict, is that there *were* people in the community "whose trust Temple ha[d] not yet won." Said Cooper in April 1981, after stating his support for the university, "You could talk to other folks that would say, 'we don't trust Temple.'"[42]

Two of the major problems in any controversial community development project arise out of a hardening of positions. First appears the utter inability to ascribe *any* bona fides to the opposition. Then comes a descent into destructive, abusive rhetoric.

For angry Temple people who felt their hearts were pure on the gentrification issue, the opposition had to be made up of political self-seekers and inner-city Huns. For SICC, their followers, and all other objectors, Temple was clearly involved once more on a 1950s- and 1960s-style real estate rampage calculated to move *them* out of their own neighborhood.

The opposition was referred to by many at Temple, in 1985, very simply as "those crazies out there,"[43] and that same opposition descended to statements about Temple's goals that were equally outrageous: "Temple is trying to build an apartheid neighborhood."[44]

On March 26, 1985, in the face of some serious community unrest, Presidents Wetzel and Liacouras, Mayor Goode, and others held a press conference on the Temple campus. There they formally announced the Bell/Temple/City partnership and the specific computer center project.

Within hours, dissident leaflets were being distributed on the streets east of Broad—just as they have been distributed on many of this nation's eastern streets ever since the eighteenth century! Two committees claimed sponsorship of the particular fliers in my possession, SICC and the Save North Philadelphia Committee. Both used similar telephone contact numbers. Some were a hurried call to arms:

Urgent! Urgent! Urgent!
EMERGENCY COMMUNITY MEETING
And you must attend—or—you may lose your apartment or home because Temple University is now expanding into our neighborhood. Temple has finished plans for big high-tech companies in our neighborhood. We must stop them before it is too late.
. . . .
We must build our neighborhood industry. We have a plan. You must get involved now!
(over for more)
This is your special invitation to come to this meeting:
Society of the Helping Church
Susquehanna and Park Avenues
Thursday, March 28th, 7:30 P.M.
Save North Philadelphia Committee
for information call 235-9079

At the March 28 meeting, a charge made was that no leaders in the community had been consulted about plans for the computer center. This charge came up again later, in a formal document that nailed Temple and Bell to the wall. The crucial issue in this connection is, who *are* the actual leaders and who *should* be consulted and when? This same issue has been known to arise when the actor is the president of the United States, and the concerned community is made up of representatives and senators.

Another flier stated: "TEMPLE TOWN IS SOCIETY HILL NORTH! 'Temple Town is an effort by Temple University and the City to take over North Philadelphia! They want to build Society Hill North! We must move out! Suburbanites will move in!"

A third exhorted: "RE-BUILD NORTH PHILLY FOR NORTH PHILADELPHIANS . . . SUPPORT COMMUNITY-BASED ECONOMIC, CULTURAL, SOCIAL AND HOUSING REBUILDING PROGRAMS . . ."[45]

The fliers contained a good deal of information on Temple's high-tech park and other Temple intentions—much, although not all of it, accurate—and many also outlined the sponsoring committee's suggestions for specific plans to "re-build the neighborhood for ourselves, not suburbanites."[46]

Notably absent from most of the fliers was any direct criticism of Bell of Pennsylvania. Generally when the telephone company is mentioned, the reference is factual, and is made in the context of the computer center being one piece among several connected with Temple's alleged plans to take over chunks of their community, to precipitate tax hikes, and ultimately to gentrify the whole neighborhood. Clearly, the focus of neighborhood anger and concern was the university, whose history of displacing community residents was now firmly back in the community consciousness.

That fact was cold comfort to the people at Bell. Their Center dreams were being attacked. Bell's original insistence that Temple and the city see to community satisfaction had obviously gone by the board. Whether their partners couldn't or wouldn't produce, the result was the same: Bell had to get out on the street on its own.

Bell executive Chuck Schalch, who had been the original coordinating force in the Smith–Liacouras-led partnerships, was by now Bell's point man for the computer center project. He picked Charles "Chuck" Powell to deal directly with the North Philadelphia community problem.

Slender, solid, and black, in his forties, Powell by 1985 had already logged some seventeen years with Bell of Pennsylvania. A native New Yorker, Powell had been a Marine Corps sergeant, a graduate of Lincoln University and the University of Pennsylvania, a high school math and social studies teacher, and a community organizer in North Philadelphia. He was also one of the telephone company's first affirmative action plan writers and implementers.

In February 1985, Powell was assigned by Schalch to a highly respected Philadelphia volunteer organization whose board of directors was, and is, made up of many of the city's most prominent persons in business, education, religion, and community development: the Urban Affairs Partnership (UAP). Powell was to continue to be paid by Bell, but to be on leave with the UAP. Exactly why this structure was chosen is not really clear, and the UAP connection was terminated within a couple of months, when the sign on his office door finally read: Charles Powell, District Manager, External Affairs, Bell of Pennsylvania. For more than two full years, Chuck Powell worked out of an office on the Temple main campus. His job was to construct hooks of mutuality on which Bell, Temple, the city, *and the community*, could hang a partnership. It is hard to see how Bell could have tapped a better person to do that work.

"I saw these North Philly folks," he told me, "as people who were left out in the sixties. Nothing ever happened for them, so they were still fighting the old sixties fights and I wanted to work with that. . . . My approach was just this: How can we make this thing work for *us*? Bell . . . hey, we're neighbors of yours, so how can we work together?"[47]

There were, of course, complications. Most arose directly out of the community, some from the obvious differences in the Bell and the Temple approaches. If community opposition is to be turned around and led to partnership, one kind of action is necessary; if political opposition is to be beaten down and conquered, that requires another. While Vice President Swygert and Tom Anderson, Temple's community relations person, were helpful to Powell with intelligence, contacts, and the like, the situation had its built-in stresses. Chuck Schalch, as close to Liacouras and other Temple personnel as he was, could be expected to reflect at least some of their perceptions, which were very often at odds with Powell's.

It is not hard to see why Temple people felt so frustrated in the face of growing local hostility: Temple was, and is, the largest employer of local workers in all of North Philadelphia, paying salaries to them of more than $20 million per year. In addition, Temple supplies millions of dollars' worth of free and under-reimbursed medical and dental care to its neighbors through its new medical center facilities (facilities constructed with scrupulous attention paid to adequate minority contractor and worker participation). Moreover, Temple provides legal aid, adult literacy programs, and a host of other human services programs to the community, as well as the use of some of its facilities.[48]

That all of this has not resulted in mutual love and trust is nevertheless not surprising. There is the reality of past sins of commission and omission. And there is the overwhelming sense of helplessness and hopelessness which Temple's neighbors must deal with continuously—and which Temple's presence has not remedied. Of course it can be, and should be, argued that it is not the university's responsibility to tend to

East of Broad Street corner. (Lewis Downey)

all of its neighbors' social ills. But that does not dismiss the question of just how sensitive the university must be to their existence, and whether, in truth, it has been sensitive enough.

There is surely community responsibility to be considered, too. If the university is a key local resource, it serves no sensible purpose to beat up on it for being behind in a game it isn't equipped to play. No university is meant to be a social welfare agency. It may have a few quite useful direct social service facilities, such as those which provide medical and dental care. But, by and large, its forte is education in the broadest sense. And help with education, in its broadest sense, is a desperately serious community need. Both basic and innovative educational processes would seem to be the most sensible starting hooks on which to hang an ongoing partnership.

In any event, in April 1985 all Bell's hopes for an early May PCC construction start came to a very abrupt end.

The land on which Bell was to build was located within an Institutional Development District (IDD). By local Philadelphia law, the Philadelphia Planning Commission is required to examine and approve any proposed revision or variance from ordinary IDD land use, and if it approves, to forward its decision to the Philadelphia City Council for the council's final approval.[49] Since construction of a four-story, 258,000-square-foot telephone company computer facility is clearly an extraordinary use in a district set aside for higher educational institutional development, a formal request for its approval was submitted to the Planning Commission in March 1985.

On April 18, 1985, the Planning Commission approved the application. On April 23, it sent a letter to that effect to the City Council president, Joseph Cole-

man, recommending that the council approve it as well. A copy of that letter was sent to District Councilman John Street.

John F. Street, councilman for North Philadelphia's 5th District, in which Temple sits, was chairman of the Council Appropriations Committee, and a member of six other committees as well. Black, outspoken, highly controversial, and politically powerful, Street had, as a younger man, attended Temple Law School. He and Peter Liacouras had apparently been good friends, but their falling out, when it came, was truly acrimonious.

Why it came is a matter of some dispute. Some maintain that it was caused by Liacouras's firing of the law school dean in office at the time he assumed the presidency. The dean was close to Street. Others say that after Street graduated, there was an issue of a long outstanding monetary debt to the law school. Whether Street owed it or not, Liacouras allegedly leaked information on the debt to the press, and that went down hard with the councilman. So much for personal past history.

I would like to have discussed these issues and others with Street. However, he alone, of all relevant parties to the PCC affair, refused to grant me an interview, despite four requests.

The prods to Councilman Street's anger were obvious enough. He saw Temple's recruitment of the Reverend Cooper's NCPA as part of a plan by Temple to defeat community action against any of their expansion plans, and even more, as a direct attack on his political base. His concerns were certainly not alleviated by the fact that neither Liacouras nor Bell (which had relied on Liacouras's assurance, on August 29, 1984, that he would have Street's support for this project) ever bothered to discuss with him directly the Bell PCC project—a project which was to be undertaken *in his councilmanic district*.[50] Commenting on the fact that he had never been consulted about the Bell-Temple plans, Street told the Philadelphia *Inquirer*:

I'm insulted when someone sends me an invitation to a press conference regarding something major in my district and no one has bothered to involve me up to that point.[51]

Further, it ought to be pointed out that in a district as contentious as his, even the powerful Street has had problems now and then holding some of his constituents in line. A flier from my files, dating back to the 1983 5th District flap over the closing of the Elverson School and the alleged sale of a nearby church, asks in bold letters:

DO YOU KNOW YOUR CHURCH MAY BE SOLD TO TEMPLE? Do you know that your pastor, Reverend Jerome Cooper and Councilman John Street may have made an agreement to sell your church to Temple University???
Ask Reverend Cooper for his honest answer.

A newspaper account of a resident march to, and meeting in, City Hall to protest the school closing relates the following story:

Parents demanded that the school be kept open, but they faced stiff opposition from their Councilman, John Street. . . . [Mrs. Taylor, a resident and a mother] claimed that the meeting quickly turned into a confrontation, during which a parent slapped Street in the face and spit at him because of what she said was his derisive attitude towards them.[52]

With regard to the Temple/Bell/City partnership, Street certainly refused to turn the other cheek.

On April 19, 1985, the day after formal Planning Commission approval of the revision of the Temple University Institutional Development District, Councilman Street wrote a letter to former friend Peter Liacouras.

The first word in that letter is "Congratulations," but to refer to that simply as a misleading opening would be to refer to the sinking of the Titanic as simply a boating mishap. After congratulating the president of Temple on his success in getting Bell to develop a new office site at 12th and Montgomery, Street got down to business. He reminded Liacouras that it was the responsibility of each councilman to support any Planning Commission recommendation affecting his district. He didn't have to say that council protocol guaranteed that if a district councilman withheld his approval, then the entire council would almost certainly withhold its legally required approval as well. Street's lack of support here would mean no building, at least in the very near future.

Street then went on to request from Temple certain documents and information which, put together, amounted to all the plans and papers, contracts, and the like related to the Bell/Temple partnership, and what Street referred to as the "Temple Master Plan for North Philadelphia." There was a final request for:

A clear concise statement of the specific benefits expected to accrue for North Philadelphia residents east of Broad Street, including types and numbers of jobs, salaries, impact on the surrounding businesses and residential community, etc.[53]

Copies of this letter were sent to eleven other persons, none of them from Bell. President Wetzel got his copy under separate cover, dated April 30, 1985.

Rodney D. Johnson, Temple vice president for Financial Affairs, composed the response for Councilman Street. It was seven pages long and had fourteen separate documents attached. Page 5 of that document contains the Temple response to how it intended to deal with community concerns "about the proposed development and to include the community in the planning process." It intended to do so through the Reverend Cooper–headed NCPA, "a strengthened

NCPA *working with, not against, the elected and public officials of the area.*"[54]

Street waited until the last possible legal moment to make his decision known to the full City Council. On May 21, 1985, he wrote to the chairman of the Rules Committee, formally requesting that the committee "disapprove the revised Temple Institutional Development District Master Plan . . . intended to permit construction of Bell Atlantic's [sic] proposed $25 million Corporate Computer Center which would be the first tenant in Temple's planned High Tech Industrial Park."[55]

He stated in his letter that he opposed the plan on eight separate grounds, all of which he listed. While the eighth contained data that was patently absurd, that is, that Bell was planning to construct a thousand-car garage, the others dealt more or less seriously with community concerns. The councilman argued that Temple's attempts to involve the community in the entire High-Tech Industrial Park process had been limited to four meetings involving a total of thirty-four people; that there had been no mass community meeting; and that

Temple has no plan to deal with the significant community opposition which stems from the concern that further development of Temple will displace more families and drive up real estate assessments without providing commensurate benefits (e.g., jobs).[56]

On May 31, 1985, Joseph E. Coleman, president of the City Council, wrote to the chairman of the Planning Commission, informing him that "the proposed Bell Development Plan recently recommended to the Council is unacceptable." The letter went on:

The Council finds that Councilman Street has not been included in the formulation of the changes made in the original [IDD] plan; nor was he involved in the planning or in preparation of local community constit-

uents which he represents and is legislatively responsible [sic].

But after formally rejecting the recommendation, the letter concluded:

Be advised and assured that this action today has nothing to do with the merit of the project itself. Council's desire and enthusiasm for this project are as high and firm as ever. We, therefore, urge immediate . . . discussion of all outstanding issues by all parties of interest.[57]

A unique and powerful partnership, committed economically and socially to an inner-city project with great potential for development, had been derailed by the very community to whom the commitment was directed. While a politician's personal pique surely played a role, even more so did the related failure of the partnership to heed local history, and to address substantial community issues sensibly. Getting the PCC and the High Tech Park back on track surely depended on Bell's handling those same community issues sensibly now, and in the face of John Street's setting the agenda.

To begin with, the councilman refused to deal with Liacouras, or anyone else at Temple, in any way at all. The only Bell representative he deigned to recognize was President Gilbert Wetzel. Even given that he had a legitimate personal complaint about having been bypassed, and a legitimate political complaint about not having had the chance to deal with his constituents' concerns, Street's summer-of-'85 intransigence was both unreasonable and destructive.

Bell did not do well to rely heavily on Temple advice concerning John Street in the first place, but there *was* evidence available to the councilman of the telephone company's bona fides. Even given his legitimate concern about tax hikes and subsequent gentrification, the very decision to locate such a sensitive, expensive operation in North Philadelphia deserved more positive weight than Street ever gave it on his scales.

Bell early in 1985 had gone to the Urban Affairs Partnership for help in effectuating their overall determination to benefit the community surrounding the computer center. The UAP, which for years has been concerned about inner-city problems, functions mainly as a conscience and a catalyst for the Philadelphia corporate community. Through its broad-based board and its working staff, headed by Managing Partner James Bodine and Deputy Director (and former state senator) Phil Price, it works to direct corporate attention, effort, and resources to key areas of need, such as public education, youth employment, and housing.[58] In connection with the Bell North Philadelphia commitment, Gil Wetzel was elected to the UAP board of directors in early 1985.

Bell had also charged its outside firm construction manager for the Corporate Computer Center with putting together a Minority Participation Program to guarantee minority bidding and work on the construction project.[59]

Councilman Street nevertheless chose to proceed on the supposition that the only way to deal with Bell was to assume the role of potentate and treat it with disdain. As a result, June and July negotiations were, for the most part, a true midsummer madness.

Street refused to deal with Chuck Schalch despite his obvious clout as a Bell-Temple middleman. Perhaps he felt the Bell executive was tainted by his links to Temple. In any event, since everyone else involved in continuing negotiations *did* rely on Schalch as the conduit, Schalch took to staying close to a mobile phone in order to hear the latest from Temple and Bell personnel, the mayor's office, the council, and the city Commerce Department.

"It was fantastic," Schalch recalled. "When I did

get the chance to be on the golf course, I'd get called off for phone calls four times in an afternoon. We had construction bids out, prices were ready to go up, we had to be ready to move from two other buildings. Just imagine the pressure on everybody."[60] And nobody ever knew exactly what the councilman really wanted.

"There was talk around," Gil Wetzel told me, "that Street was attempting to extort money for himself, or for his law firm or whatever, but he never tried to extort anything from me. Never."[61]

Well, then, exactly what *did* Street demand?

"In fact," said Wetzel, "there were times when it was clear that he didn't think Bell *could* do much for his constituency: 'If you train 'em, they'll leave this community,' kind of remark. What was he looking for? Bottom line: Solve all the problems of North Philadelphia . . . [for example] get the banks of Philadelphia to give us low percentage mortgages.[62] There was reason to believe during that long, hot summer that Street did not really want to see Peter Liacouras get his high-tech park at all, and that, therefore, there should be *no* agreement with Bell.

The most astonishing personality performance of 1985 regarding the PCC, however, was not that of Councilman John Street. It was that of Bell President Gilbert Wetzel.

Twice in June, Street arranged community meetings at which the chief executive was to serve as the recipient of complaints arising out of a generation of hurt and anger. Despite strong senior management support for the North Philadelphia Computer Center concept by early 1985, that same management's objection to Wetzel's personal meetings with Street were also strong, and there was insistence that he go into any North Philadelphia on-site meeting only with bodyguards.[63] Wetzel refused, and attended the first encounter with Chuck Schalch.

The meeting was held at 17th Street and Columbia Avenue in back of the first-floor office of 47th Ward Leader, Herbert Arlene.[64] The community group present was not large. Paula Brown Taylor, Shirley Kitchen, and several others made up an activist team that had to work its way through a good deal of personal and collective fury before any meaningful negotiations could begin.

"This was the first time we ever had the president of a big corporation come into our community to talk to us," Paula Brown Taylor recalled. "We used the first meeting to vent our anger. About why Bell used Temple to deal with our community, about a lot of things. Some of them really not Bell, you know. Bell basically got beat up on, got flack, for Temple and for the city, too, I guess. We'd been jerked around before, and we were angry."[65]

The confrontational meeting was a first for corporate President Wetzel, too. He heard shouting and recriminations, complaints about past wrongs and frustrations with which he and his company had no direct connection. Poverty, joblessness, and a general lack of access to an economy that experts insisted had nowhere to go but up for everyone else, seemed to trigger the strongest resentment. Wetzel watched shouters very close to his face and he saw not only anger, but fear. Fear more closely connected to the building path Bell of Pennsylvania and Temple were embarked upon. He listened patiently, convincing them finally that this CEO had come to their turf not to try to bully or threaten but, truly, to listen.

Then Wetzel attempted to deal with one of their major concerns by promising to help with jobs for local residents on the computer center construction site, and with training where qualifications for jobs might be lacking.[66] But he also reminded them that Bell couldn't wait forever and that if some cooperative agreement wasn't reached, the PCC might be forced to go elsewhere.[67]

The second June community meeting was less confrontational. Wetzel's willingness to hear them out had impressed the activists and the community residents they had reported back to in follow-up meetings held in halls and local churches east of Broad Street. But their demands, though less strident, were hardly tempered by cool judgment. Bell of Pennsylvania was big and rich, after all, so why not get right out front with a long community wish list? So, although some sensible requests were debated—a possible nonprofit community development corporation which could be a spearhead for local development, for example—for the most part demands were presented that could not be met.[68] Wetzel reiterated calmly that he was willing to consider *reasonable* requests, but he presented a mixed warning and plea: time could run out on us all.

The question for most people at Bell was not, how well did the chief do up there, but rather: Why should he put himself through this at all? Why not just take our Center somewhere else?

Days and weeks droned on with community dissidents still up in arms, and Street holding up the city council. Larry Momarella of Bell Real Estate was weighed down with concerns, and his main one was this: The original construction schedule had allowed for all cement to be poured *before* winter. Now they would certainly have to pour some in below freezing weather, meaning much higher costs to keep areas warm, not to mention inconvenience.[69] And of course, planning with Parsons and the outside team went on, yet contracts could not be let.

Not one Bell employee interviewed in 1987 could explain why Gil Wetzel had maintained Bell's commitment to North Philadelphia in the face of the resistance Bell encountered. I looked forward to asking him, because there was even more for Bell of Pennsylvania's CEO to deal with than the direct confrontation with hostile community people, and political delay.

John Street informed Wetzel that he was willing to meet on a one-to-one basis, to discuss some sort of compromise on the variance needed for the PCC to go forward. Wetzel was willing, and the question became: Where would the meetings take place? There was the president's office, of course, or the councilman's at City Hall. But neither fit John Street's bill. Street was a jogger and he requested a set-up whereby he could run and play royalty at the same time. They would meet at dusk in a dimly lit rendezvous: a shaded path by Philadelphia's Boathouse Row along East River Drive.[70] Wetzel agreed to, and did, attend two such conferences in the hope of coming to some sensible solution. While the issues discussed were of possible corporate and community mutual benefit, the two men, standing in the shadows by the water's edge, were telling testimony of two very different personal agendas.

By late June, Mayor Goode and his then Director of Commerce David Brenner were discussing the phenomenon of this extraordinary corporate CEO, who somehow felt personally committed to hang in with the North Philadelphia community undertaking, despite pressure, procrastination, and personal affronts. Their attitude was, God bless him, but for heaven's sake, why?[71] And, of course, for how long?

By early July, the newspapers were covering the story of the Bell computer center delay.[72] Wilson Goode was on the telephone regularly with each of his major players: an angry Peter Liacouras, who was convinced the mayor wasn't doing enough; an angry John Street, who was convinced he was doing too much; and an anxious Gil Wetzel, who, in addition to being soothed generally had somehow to be persuaded to keep his investment inside Philadelphia, even if North Philadelphia couldn't be the site.

The Penn/Drexel Science Center was receptive to the idea of Bell's locating there,[73] and the mayor and his commerce director were looking at the possibility of providing Bell with alternative city sites, as well—for example, a specific open field area near the airport.[74]

Bell was toting up dollar losses, and despite his grudging admission in a newspaper interview that the PCC "idea has good potential," Street was still intransigent.[75] Some dissidents in the community appeared to have gone completely around the bend. For example, in July a North Philadelphia newspaper reported:

One banker allegedly revealed [to some community leaders] a grand plan by . . . [Philadelphia] corporations to make a spearhead into North Philadelphia's east side . . . which would open the floodgates for the entire corporated society [sic]. . . . During the Columbia Avenue meeting, personnel from Bell themselves reportedly pictured North Philadelphia as a virtual gold mine . . . which has no rival in surrounding suburbs.[76]

No treasure map was appended to that story!

By July, there was no alternative for the city or for Bell but to make an end of all this. The council president, Joe Coleman, was clearly at work to press a compromise and then a vote to approve the planning commission recommendation.[77] Mayor Goode and David Brenner went public about negotiating a non–North Philadelphia site for Bell. Temple Vice President Pat Swygert and his Community Relations Director Tom Anderson successfully went about obtaining letters of support to be sent to Wetzel, the mayor, and Joe Coleman from several key North Philadelphia organizations. In addition to NCPA, they enlisted such highly respected groups as the Norris Homes Tenant Council, the Freedom Theater, the R. W. Brown Community Center, and the National Non-Profit Corporation (with which Bell's Chuck Powell also had been working). The PCC project pressure was now pressing down on Street and dissident community people and it was clearly compromise or lose it.

There are those at Temple—and even a few at Bell—who feel that the mayor might have done more to speed up the process of compromise and ultimate agreement. He disagrees with them, of course. In our City Hall interview, Mayor Wilson Goode said that

North Philadelphia is a laboratory for testing and working on solutions for urban ills in our society everywhere. . . . High unemployment, poor housing, high crime, high school dropouts, teenage pregnancy, infant mortality . . . they have it all. What these folks need is hope. Mainly hope that a rebuilding is going to take place. For them.

Now, business and educational institutions must be a part of the growth of the city. . . . And there must be a mind-set on the part of government to realize how important it is . . . to become a catalyst for [helping them contribute to] economic development. . . . That's as much a role for government as police or fire or sanitation.

For Wilson Goode, being a catalyst does mean helping with, but not solving, sociopolitical problems that come to everyone involved with urban ills: government, private industry, and institutions of higher learning. Regarding the Bell PCC he said,

The community's response was: we want you to share some benefits with our community. . . . From my vantage point that conflict was a blessing in disguise because all of us came away knowing more about how to begin some movement toward resolution, toward giving people hope, and not just struggling along as a target of resentment.

I tried to keep things moving, to balance Liacouras and Street, to interpret for, and to encourage Wetzel. In the course of that problem, we discussed alterna-tive sites with some, and with others the fact that if it couldn't be Temple, the city was likely to lose the computer center. Without that leverage being applied [this situation] wouldn't have worked itself out as it did.

The mayor concluded, "Gil Wetzel, in my view, showed tremendous courageous leadership throughout all of this . . . to make the statement of faith he did in North Philadelphia."[78]

Wetzel's faith was still being sorely tested. All the community people, east and west of Broad Street, who were still fighting against Temple and Bell had banded together in the organization they called the East of Broad Coalition. Darryl Taylor (no relation to Paula Brown Taylor), a thirty-ish black activist, joined that group early on.

"We had weekly community meetings on the gentrification and tax base issues mainly," he said when interviewed.

We weren't about to deal with another big development push by Temple without a fight. We were coming off some earlier talk, too, about Temple buying a church at Broad and Susquehanna and tearing that black church down.

You have to remember the history. Temple had some community people working with them, and we tried talking with Tom Anderson and others at the school— the Coalition did. But we perceived Temple as playing community groups off against one another.[79]

In their frustration, the East of Broad Coalition group had appeared at the Philadelphia Planning Commission to contest the Institutional Development District variances, had met with the mayor once, and with John Street many times. They were the ones who helped set up, and attended, the two Wetzel-Bell community meetings. They were not about to give up now, even with the pressure on. Still, something specific had to be done when it became clear that City Council President Coleman, in the absence of a negotiated resolution, was going to call for a full council vote in order to push the Bell computer center variance through.[80]

Such a "winning" vote would not, of course, guarantee future peace for Bell of Pennsylvania or for its computer building. In the Charette period turmoil, it must be remembered, community members had thrown themselves in front of bulldozers working on Temple development land! But the vote surely would spell defeat for the opposition attempt to keep the computer center out and reduce their position to that of inner-city snipers, rather than partners in a positive cause.

It was at this point in mid-July that an unusual agreement was developed. The East of Broad Coalition leadership decided to put some basic demands in writing that would bind Bell, Temple, the city, and the community together to accomplish specific results. Paula Brown Taylor, Shirley Kitchen, and Darryl Taylor played a major role in sketching out what should be in the document. What the community had to give was its full cooperation. The question was: how much could they get? They reduced their demands to the three basic areas of jobs, job training, and a vehicle for general community development—a specific new community development corporation (CDC).

"The Coalition was the source of the written agreement idea," Paula Brown Taylor says. "We drafted one and then John Street 'lawyered' it. Got it down on paper in the proper way. What we did was, we had community meetings. There was a church at Broad and Dolphin then that we used a lot as one place to get together and ask community folk what they thought. You know, like what do you think ought to be in a written agreement? We got feedback, we put it down, and John Street drew up the formal agree-

ment. We didn't want to sign it. We didn't feel we had the authority."[81]

The Coalition wanted Temple included, but as Darryl Taylor recalls, Temple found the CDC a particular sticking point because Temple wanted to set up its own group as the major east of Broad Street leadership.

With Temple refusing outright to become involved in any settlement with the East of Broad Coalition, the final partnership document, though benefiting the university, was signed only by Bell of Pennsylvania, the City of Philadelphia, and the councilman representing the Fifth Councilmanic District of the city. It took the form of a Memorandum of Understanding, and it reads as follows:

MEMORANDUM OF UNDERSTANDING

This Memorandum of Understanding entered into by and between the City of Philadelphia (hereinafter "City"), the Bell Telephone Company of Pennsylvania (hereinafter "Bell of PA") and the Councilman for the Fifth Councilmanic District of the City of Philadelphia (hereinafter "Councilman") for the benefit of the community surrounding Temple University.

WHEREAS *Temple University has proposed the development of a High-Tech Industrial Park adjacent to the Temple University main campus; and*

WHEREAS *Bell of PA plans to be the first tenant of the High-Tech Industrial Park upon completion of construction of a computer center building on a site at the northeast corner of 12th Street and Montgomery Avenue; and*

WHEREAS *in the community surrounding Temple University, i.e., the area bounded by Girard Avenue on the south, Lehigh Avenue on the north, 22nd Street on the west and Front Street on the east (hereinafter "community"), there exists a substantial amount of sub-standard and vacant housing and a* high unemployment rate among members of the labor force; and

WHEREAS there is concern that development of new physical facilities without thoughtful comprehensive planning has the tendency to increase property values in the area, thereby increasing property tax liabilities, and has the potential, therefore, to result in displacement of low and moderate income residents from their homes and neighborhood; and

WHEREAS it is more likely that community support for this future High-Tech Industrial Park development will be forthcoming if the community is made a participant and a co-beneficiary of the development; and

WHEREAS successful development of High-Tech industries in Philadelphia, both on and off Temple's campus, will require a skilled labor force; and

WHEREAS Bell of PA, and the City of Philadelphia desire to cooperate in a comprehensive effort to revitalize the area in a way which benefits and involves the community as well as institutions.

ACCORDINGLY

I. With respect to Bell of PA's corporate computer center (hereinafter "the Facility") to be constructed at 12th Street and Montgomery Avenue, Philadelphia, Bell will use its best efforts (a) to arrange for the independent construction contractors involved in the construction of the facility to cooperate in an effort to reach a goal that 25% of all construction jobs on the site be filled with qualified (including organized labor affiliation where required) Community residents and (b) thereafter, to obtain for available positions, in accordance with Bell's hiring practices, and consistent with its established equal opportunity and minority business commitments, 10 to 15 qualified (including organized labor affiliation where required) Community residents each year at the facility, until the number of qualified community residents so employed constitutes and continues to constitute—consistent with Bell's employment practices and applicable labor agreements—approximately 25% of the work force at the facility.

II. The City shall initiate and Bell of PA shall cooperate in establishing a job training program the goal of which shall be the preparation of eventually up to 300 Community residents, including Blacks, Hispanics and women for the high-tech jobs as they become available in the Park. As new businesses locate in the Area, Bell of PA and the City will seek their participation in providing training programs related to the job opportunities which they will make available for Community residents.

III. The City shall initiate and Bell of PA shall cooperate in the establishment of a Community Development Corporation to service that part of the community located east of Broad Street and shall further provide substantial technical assistance to the Community Development Corporation.

IV. The City shall initiate and Bell of PA shall cooperate to promote a scholarship fund to benefit worthy students residing in the community, the criteria for which will be established by the parties.

V. The City shall initiate and Bell of PA shall cooperate in raising the sum of $2,000,000 for the development plan for the part of the community located east of Broad Street. Said funding shall be separate and apart from the City's commitment to spend $5,000,000 of city funds in the "North Philadelphia" area.

VI. The Mayor of the City, the President and Chief Executive Officer of Bell of PA and the Fifth District Councilman shall tour that part of the community located east of Broad Street with residents of that area and representatives of community groups in that area.

VII. The Mayor of the City, and the President of Bell of PA shall attend a mass meeting of community residents at the NU-TEC Theatre on a date to be determined to explain the provisions of this

Memorandum of Understanding to Community residents.

Dated this 7 day of August, 1985

City of Philadelphia
By Wilson Goode
Mayor

The Bell Telephone Company of Pennsylvania
By Gilbert H. Wetzel
President and Chief Executive Officer

Fifth Councilmanic District of
The City of Philadelphia
By John Street
Councilman

The key whereases are the fifth, related to the community's participation and co-beneficiary position regarding development, and the last, related to the benefit and involvement of the community, as well as of the participating institutions. These provisions could be fitted into any inner-city partnership development effort, anywhere, where higher taxes and gentrification are at issue.

No single dissident group or coalition should ever sign for "the community" of course, as none did here. The community's duly elected and confirmed representative must do that. It is irrelevant that he or she might be too pugnacious or too egomaniacal or too whatever else—irrelevant, that is, if we intend to stand behind the democratic process.

For the community, the signatures of Bell and the city represented a sincere best-efforts promise to provide some jobs and job training, some education, and community development benefits, together with backing for an east of Broad Street community development corporation to help service that specific neighborhood. For Bell and the city, the councilman's signature meant a joint venture, holding out the promise of continued community backing and support.

There were no guarantees for mutual growth in this August 7, 1985, document. But certainly there was a positive ending and, equally important, a clean beginning—at least for Bell, if not for Temple.

One large question still looms over the events leading up to August 7, 1985: Why, in the face of real alternatives, had Bell of Pennsylvania's chief executive officer persevered?

As a former New York City commissioner in the late sixties and early seventies who had faced some community confrontations of my own, I asked Gil Wetzel: "Since you had other sites available for building—places where you would have been welcomed—why did you take so much personally and still keep on? You're the CEO of a tremendous corporation. Sure, there was a real commitment that you and Ray Smith shared. But isn't there a point where you just say, 'Who the hell needs this? I've done enough. I'm just going to pack it in?'"

"Sure," he said. "When any final deadline I've worked out isn't met, and from then on the corporation is truly hurt. That's enough."

"I don't mean that," I told him. "I assume you figured structural costs and benefits to your shareholders in all good faith, and to protect their interests you'd hold to a pre-set deadline. But how about a limit to your *personal* costs before you reach that point?"

It seemed to me from the look on his face that he'd not discussed this subject before—at least not outside his own house. He thought a bit, but didn't take too long to answer.

It's not complicated. I said to myself: if this was the right thing to do originally, it still is. . . . The objective was the permit, the OK to build . . . so . . . as far as these meetings with Street, well, if that's what it took to reach it . . . why worry about where you talk, or if you do it while John's jogging? You don't dump a corporation's best interests, or a community's, for the sake of your own ego . . . I don't say I never thought about that. . . . Here's some ego for you: I thought, I've taken positions before and not given way and I'm damned if I will now. . . . My wife says I'm stubborn. I say I'm persistent. As for the community meetings I went to, a CEO has to know what's happening in the community out there—that's walking around management. [82]

Later, I had occasion to read a short piece Wetzel wrote for a business publication on the subject of "corporate citizenship." In an age of hostile takeover snatch-and-grabbers, other short-term gimme-mine-right-now profiteers, self-interested golden parachuters, and economic dog-eat-dog tenured professor theorists, this CEO's article is a breath of unpolluted air.

Wetzel argues in the article that companies should be good citizens because their consciences compel them to be, not just because it pays. "The public," he writes from experience, "has little tolerance for being patronized." Which is not to say that being a good corporate citizen doesn't pay:

Since vibrant and healthy communities offer us the greatest potential for installing new lines and selling . . . services . . . Bell of Pennsylvania is most interested in helping all of the communities we serve fulfill their promise.

But, he reminds us,

economic health is only one ingredient of the Quality of Life Formula which makes a community prosperous and desirable. Exxon Chairman C. C. Gavin once said, 'It doesn't make sense to talk about successful corporations in a society whose schools, hospitals, churches, symphonies or libraries are deteriorating.'

Wetzel has no problem dealing with ethics and personal responsibility:

A company's motives reflect not only upon the character of the company itself, but also upon the character of its managers—from the CEO down. People, not companies, decide ethical questions. And the personal standards of those charged with managing Bell of Pennsylvania or any other company—our sense of honor, if you will—are reflected by the motives governing our corporate citizenship. At stake is no less than our legacy. . . . Ultimately, posterity will judge present day managers—most of all the CEO—based upon the character of the company we leave behind and its contribution to society. [83]

This manager's, and his company's, perseverance through the summer of 1985 is not so hard to understand after all. Such behavior does make it somewhat more difficult to tolerate the argument that a corporation's only social responsibility is to make quickly as much profit for its stockholders as it can and still stay out of court.

Once the Agreement among Bell, the city, and the community had been signed, the City Council approved the Planning Commission variance recommendation and the PCC was on its way.

Since actual building construction presented the first opportunity, subsequent to the August Agreement, for Bell to demonstrate its good faith to the community, a partner with how-best-to-do-it experience was needed. Bell turned to the Philadelphia Urban Coalition and its director, Ernest Jones.

The Coalition, a nonprofit agency, had been founded in 1968, following inner-city disturbances occurring in the wake of the murder of Martin Luther King, Jr. It grew from being a channeler of corporate resources to communities for economic development purposes, to being a provider of job training and development and support services for minority businesses. Earlier in the 1980s, the Coalition had been awarded a contract by Temple to help the university involve minorities and women in the construction of its new hospital and medical center. While fifteen to seventeen percent participation was normal for the Philadelphia area, the Coalition, working with Turner Construction Company, achieved a level of thirty-two percent minority and five percent female subcontractors, and thirty-seven percent black and female workers on the Temple job.[84]

With John Street's blessing,[85] Bell and the Urban Coalition went about involving neighborhood people in the PCC building process. In the signed Memorandum of Understanding, Bell promised only to use its best efforts to employ community residents for twenty-five percent of all construction jobs—nothing at all was said about minority and women's business enterprise involvement. Nevertheless, since Bell was interested in creating employment opportunites for community residents, and in enhancing community relations, it was willing, through the Philadelphia Urban Coalition, to formulate a plan of action based on the general public perception of what they were expected to do, rather than on the strict terms of the written memorandum.

A serious game was underway now, and both Bell and the PUC were lucky to have, as their quarterback, James A. Roundtree. As project director of the Philadelphia Urban Coalition minority- and women-based Employment Construction Project, Roundtree is not a man to be taken lightly on or off a construction job. At first glance, this big man in his thirties appears to be about eight feet tall. Actually he's closer to six feet ten, but as he comes at you directly the difference is more or less insignificant. A sign on the desk in his office reads: "Be kind to me, I'm having a rotten day." As an enticement to good behavior from visitors, it's

utterly superfluous. It's not that Roundtree necessarily comes on strong—he certainly didn't to me. It's just that one naturally wishes to avoid responsibility for creating any situation where he might.

After college, Roundtree played pro basketball in and around South America for a while, returned in 1977 to the United States, and went to work for the PUC.

"Bell was gung-ho to go ahead with this project," he told me, "and they wanted an on-the-job guy to be sure that all went well. We, of course, have had experience."[86]

Roundtree and the Philadelphia Urban Coalition had, for three years, been inventorying the entire construction business, together with the number of minorities and women in the building trades. It became pretty clear that they couldn't find enough card-carrying, skilled tradespeople in the North Philadelphia area to staff twenty-five percent of all the jobs. But surely laborers could be placed. The Coalition wrote language into all Bell bids encouraging local community hiring, and then, with the cooperation of the contractors, began assigning slots. Prime contractors contacted trade unions to get what skilled people they could from the community, for example, plumbers and steamfitters, and if that were not possible, to use locals in apprentice programs.

"The electrical contractors, especially, were great," Roundtree emphasized. "And we placed more than sixty local people on the construction job at one time or another. Roughly thirty percent of the workforce was minority or female—and twenty-two percent of all skilled trade slots to boot. We're proud of something else: We didn't just place, and monitor compliance—we stayed on it. All but three of the locals hired are still in the construction trades. Eight or ten are only seasonals, but several are permanent. We try to promote careers, not jobs."[87]

The East of Broad Coalition leaders who had led

the fight resulting in the Memorandum of Understanding had submitted a list of more than one hundred names of locals seeking jobs to the PUC, and they wanted only east of Broad residents working there.[88] They could not, of course, get all they wanted.

"We took a lot of heat to demonstrate [to the East of Broad community] the legitimacy of this project," Roundtree said. But he understands where community pugnaciousness comes from. "Five or fifteen percent unemployment's just a figure if you're working. It's always one hundred percent when you aren't. . . . There were a lot of ups and downs with the community, but the Building Trades Council, the Urban Coalition, contractors, and Bell worked together. We had meetings once a month, that kind of thing, and so it worked. It says a lot for that community that so many of their folks are still working, too."[89]

There was no way, of course, that Bell alone could have managed the construction and community job satisfaction problem. Nor could the Philadelphia Urban Coalition have managed it alone. It took Bell's good faith and commitment, and weekly meetings with Jones and Roundtree, together with PUC's expertise.[90]

While construction of the computer center building moved along, Chuck Powell, Bell's man-in-the-street, was hard at work promoting continued Bell and community cooperation, both generally and with specific projects. The important project related to the job training program paragraph in the August 7 Memorandum was a joint cooperative effort by Bell, Temple, the City Housing Authority Tenant Council, and the Benjamin Franklin Partnership (which provides funding for projects promoting high-tech development in North Philadelphia).

The corporation, the university, and the city—with encouragement and advice from the Urban Affairs Partnership—developed, funded, and undertook the operation of the Norris Homes Career Mobility Center. That center was to be the first job preparation program to be located at a public housing project in Philadelphia, and surely the first to be sponsored directly by a private business firm.[91]

The Norris Homes Housing Project itself is located close by the Temple main campus, hardly more than a block away from the Bell computer center building. The Career Mobility Center focus was not merely to find some kind of job for a few of the residents (the majority of whom were unemployed), but rather, "to provide career exploration, guidance, and job readiness training to lead displaced and disadvantaged workers into careers in today's job market."[92]

Seymour Rosenthal, director of the Temple School of Social Administration's Center for Social Policy and Community Development, which runs the Mobility Center, says that it was birthed as the result of Bell's efforts. "We were going to be working with low-income people," he said, "who don't have the supports we do. So they go from job to job if they can, but they've no career to go to or from. Therefore, this program was set up to provide social, education, and job readiness support—not to be a specific jobs skills program."[93]

With Bell community liaison support from Chuck Powell, Bell executive staff support from Chuck Schalch, and a Bell corporation donation of $30,000, the Career Mobility Center opened its doors on October 16, 1985, under Rosenthal's and Temple's guidance.

Meanwhile, at Bell headquarters, an internal interdepartmental team had been formed to monitor PCC and neighborhood progress in the areas of construction, community relations and program development, and positive publicity. Operating under the direction of Chuck Schalch, the group met twice in 1985, in October and November. While External Affairs and

Community Relations people dominated, Real Estate, ISO, Personnel, Purchasing, and Law were also present. Together they were called Bell's "Temple Project" group.

The Memorandum of Understanding of August 7 was the clearest statement Bell could make that it no longer depended on Temple, but rather assumed responsibility for its own successes or failures in the PCC community. The new in-house group was a sensible, constructive corporate recognition of the fact that Bell of Pennsylvania's community responsibility was ongoing, and that mutual growth demanded constant oversight and nurturing.

Four areas received attention at the two interdepartmental group meetings in 1985.

The first was construction, and by and large the news was good. Overall, by November 5, the work on the building was proceeding two weeks ahead of schedule. The only problem was that some concrete would have to be poured during the difficult winter months, perhaps as late as the following February.

The second area had to do with short- and long-range goals for community development. There were Real Estate and External Affairs reports on Bell/PUC/union progress with minority and neighborhood hiring, and on Norris Homes Center progress as well. Chuck Powell was on the street a good deal of the time, working together both with individuals, such as Kitchen and Brown, and with organizations like the National Temple Non-Profit corporation—the community housing developer.[94] Powell outlined his future strategy for the interdepartmental team: To identify opportunities for Bell development initiatives in community development programming, and to match those opportunities to corporate community goals and available budget and strategic considerations. There would have to be a concomitant development of measurable, performance-based evaluation criteria for all program investments.

The third group focus was on how best, and when, to communicate progress externally as well as internally—for example, through use of the media.

But it was a fourth area, connected somewhat to all the rest, which pointed up a central Bell dilemma: The Memorandum of Understanding issue of the hiring of community people to work in the computer center facility.[95] Bell's own October 1, 1985, "Computer Operations Force Projection Summary" showed that while the 1985 Wayne and Schuylkill computer centers' combined staff of 216 persons would reach a peak of 237 in 1987—through migration overlap—still, by 1989, permanent shrinkage would bring the total down to 195.[96]

Councilman Street was quite aware of the PCC's employment limits, and said so early on, in writing. His May 21, 1985, letter to the City Council rules committee chairman, requesting disapproval of the IDD variance, gave as a reason:

No new jobs would be created by the transfer of Bell['s] operation to the Temple site; therefore, new jobs would not be created for community residents.[97]

Still, all in all, the corporate–higher education–government–community partnership was in fairly good shape as 1985 drew to a close. Not only was Bell's building rising, but the Philadelphia Gas Works, emboldened by the Bell commitment, was getting involved in the area through the construction of a new building and parking lot at 9th and Columbia Avenue. The Norris Homes Career Mobility Center now had begun to enroll people. Bell of Pennsylvania had even moved forward on Paragraph IV of the Memorandum of Understanding regarding the creation of a scholarship fund "to benefit worthy students residing in the community." Chuck Schalch reported in November that Bell, working in concert with actor Bill Cosby, would be contributing $50,000 to a Camille Cosby Scholarship Fund.[98]

For Temple, the High-Tech Park had at last begun to take shape. The city had not lost an important investment. And the community had joined in a partnership that, for once, might show it a profit. Exactly what kind of partnership and what kind of profit remained to be seen.

Clearly the war was over. But, as the world has seen since 1945, peace isn't always comfortable. Also, peace takes a lot of work to maintain and, by itself, does not guarantee growth for everybody. Nevertheless, as 1986 and 1987 in North Philadelphia would show, building peace can be exciting.

Basement of Philadelphia Computer Center. (Nona Short)

3

PEACE
AND
PROGRESS
THROUGH
INTERDEPENDENCE

Nineteen eighty-six was a year for building. A physical structure would have to rise on a special parcel of land. And a partnership for economic and social progress would have to grow up out of an unusual Memorandum of Understanding.

By March, electrical contractors were wiring the Bell of Pennsylvania computer center at 11th and Montgomery Streets, and the steel wall was ready to go up. By the end of April some of the glass sliding panels were in place. By June, sixty percent of the building's heat-treated, mirrored-glass outside curtain was up, and work was starting on the third floor. By October 1, construction was in its final stages with floors, wall coverings, even paintings about ready to

be installed. Before the month was out, ten thousand square feet would be ready to be occupied by the first Bell employees. Union agreements for some of the construction workers had come up for negotiation on May 1, but neither slowdown nor strike resulted. Work proceeded apace, and the weather could not have been better.[1]

Bell's ISO and Real Estate people had done a remarkable planning, bid-processing, and oversight job. They had a fine construction manager and some good contractors and union people to work with. And, unlike the late sixties and early seventies when Temple had expanded, community people had not caused delays by actually throwing themselves in front of contractor bulldozers! That did not happen

79

here with Bell, because the 1985 struggle with the community had been cooperatively resolved; because Bell honestly wanted to help out with jobs; and because, with the Urban Coalition at work, there was a process for promoting community cooperation and construction progress and for dissipating community heat.

Jim Roundtree interviewed all the minority people who showed up asking for employment in order to determine the true extent of their skills and the degree of their commitment to hard work. Throughout the entire construction period, he and his people maintained intensive day-to-day contact with contractors and workers on the site to be sure everything continued to go well. In November 1985, fourteen percent of the personnel on the construction site (54 people) were from the North Philadelphia community. Fifty-two percent were minorities and women.[2] By the time the building and the parking garage located on the same lot were completed in 1987, out of a total work force of 731, 286 workers had been minorities and women and 68 of them were from the contiguous community.[3]

Even with that remarkable record, the East of Broad Coalition—the group that had fought the hardest throughout 1985—was not satisfied. Only 16 of the community's 68 workers had come from *their* list of people. Theirs was partly a concern for the organization's status, but they also felt that "community" for the purpose of construction jobs meant the East of Broad Street zip code area only. They vented their anger over this, but it never affected the construction work. This was because the bottom line was dialogue, not threats or violence, and the Urban Coalition and Bell's Chuck Powell were there to talk with. Most important, they were there to take for Bell and Temple whatever community heat was generated. In the end, the overall feeling certainly was that the community

had been treated fairly by a decent and responsible partner.

But, beyond construction, Bell had to deal with a basic mistake that cast a shadow over partnership progress. Paragraph I.b of the Memorandum of Understanding called for Bell to hire "10 to 15 qualified . . . community residents each year at the facility" until they comprised twenty-five percent of the entire PCC work force.

That, of course, was impossible, and the people at Bell knew it, just as John Street had known it from the very beginning.[4] The PCC was a high-tech resident in a contemplated high-tech park, surrounded by a low-tech/no-tech labor pool. It would help not one whit to stand up now and say: None of you are "qualified," so please just go away! It was a little too late for that.

Pressured mainly by Paragraph I.b and community expectations, and then by Chuck Schalch, who felt Bell had somehow to come through in a "crucial situation,"[5] a frustrated Information Systems Organization, responsible for organizing and operating the PCC, squirmed and twisted, and Bell personnel people sweated it out. Harry Artz of ISO, and Lou Walls, top assistant to Bell's district manager of Affirmative Action Charles Ashley, agreed first to assign one programmer basic training slot to a North Philadelphia resident. All over Bell, people scrambled to find a way to fit decent, willing, but untrained and technically unqualified people into state-of-the-art, high-technology slots.

When the center opened, according to Lou Walls of Bell's Personnel Division, "Newspaper articles stated things like 'Two hundred jobs exist at the Bell PCC' and 'Fifty will be coming from the community.' We were overwhelmed. We had a groundswell of nonmanagement job seekers—and we'd already had seventy-five community applicants for jobs there six months before the computer center even opened."[6]

Basement of Philadelphia Computer Center. (Nona Short)

What the fledgling Bell of Pennsylvania and North Philadelphia community partners were dealing with now was the unhappiness that almost always results from a confusion of means with ends or, more pointedly, from a confusion of the 'how to's' with the 'what's.' Nowhere do we Americans do this better (or worse) than in the high-technology area.

Norbert Wiener, mathematical genius, cyberneticist supreme, and an insightful human being, wrote nearly forty years ago, in reference to the dawning computer age, that we Americans had better be careful to place the proper emphasis on such technological advancement. Knowing *how to do things*, he felt, was something we were astonishingly good at. But, for Wiener, the key to human progress lay elsewhere. This came from knowing *what our purposes ought to be*—and that, he said, we Americans were very bad at.[7]

Applied to the North Philadelphia partnership, one short-term end—one immediate 'what'—was meaningful community participation and benefit—participation that would satisfy the human need to put bread on the table and bolster self-respect. But the PCC was not the specific 'how to' to accomplish this. It was itself the key immediate 'what,' the 'what' best translated as *hope*. Without the presence of hope, there can be no effective partnership at all in the inner city.

Yet in an age where sophisticated information is synonymous with economic survival, how does one deal with inner-city people who neither possess it, nor have sufficient access to systems and institutions that do? If the dazzling information utilization center in North Philadelphia *is* to represent hope rather than to stand as a wretched reminder of technical ignorance and consequent impossibilities, then some 'how to's' surely must be found to remedy basic deficiencies. The Temple High-Tech Park will be one important 'how to,' but nevertheless only one.

In any inner-city partnership, the key 'how to' for every 'what'—one crucial means to every end—is surely *education*. That is a sufficiently complex matter, all by itself, to warrant fuller discussion further on.

Bell of Pennsylvania's Chuck Powell spent almost all of 1986 and 1987 forging partnership links with the community, which, with the help of Jim Roundtree and Ernest Jones of the Urban Coalition, included the provision of construction site jobs. But the most important, most demanding task, requiring the bringing together of many groups, involved Paragraph III of the Memorandum of Understanding: A Community Development Corporation had to be established to service the East of Broad community.

Community Development Corporations (CDCs) are incorporated nonprofit groups made up of local community people, engaged basically in neighborhood housing and commercial and industrial activities, with their goal being economic development. In 1986, twenty-two such CDCs were members of the overall Community Development Corporation, Inc., of Philadelphia. Some purchased and rehabilitated residence and commercial properties, others ran day-care centers for minority working mothers, while others operated fast-food franchises and one even operated a recycling factory.[8]

The two problems common to most CDCs are politics and operations, and neither is easy to manage. The politics begins with the issue of control: Just which people from which associated community groups should actually control and manage the CDC? Operational concerns start with the skills required to manage and conduct business successfully after leadership is chosen. The East of Broad *Coalition*, which aimed to become the East of Broad CDC, presented both problems clearly. There was concern about who should make up the leadership, and the Memorandum of Understanding itself highlighted the skills issue by calling, in Paragraph III, for "substantial technical assistance to the [new] Community Development Corporation."

The question of whether the "best" people in a fractured community end up running a CDC depends a good deal on one's point of view about what "best" means. All inner-city communities are, to some extent, fractured (that is, they have combative status and power groupings). A scarcity of real power, perks, and riches seems to encourage that situation. But then there are also the American wars for corporate control. An abundance of real power, perks, and riches seems to encourage that situation.

It might be argued that for-profit corporate battles are different from community disputes since their rewards have nothing to do with public monies, a constantly diminishing amount of which does help to fund CDCs. That argument is hardly impressive in the light of Chrysler, U.S. savings banks and such—not to mention creative corporate use of the Federal Tax Code and Chapter 11 debtor proceedings. The East of Broad people were no exception to the rule that the scent of prestige, power, and prizes tends to disrupt coalitions. This rule bears no relationship to the color of one's skin, or to one's accent, or to the amount of assets one possesses.

Some of the people interviewed in connection with the East of Broad CDC seemed to feel that "John Street's people" won out in a community where coalitions abounded; in the end, politics prevailed, even at the expense of competence. That argument seems disingenuous. At any rate, others interviewed felt just as strongly that the capacity to coordinate politics successfully and to rally elected political power to support one's cause was, in fact, one indication of competence. At a minimum, it shows the possession of an important community development skill not necessarily birthed through the medium of "substantial technical assistance."

None of which is meant to suggest that a Community Development Corporation can be a success if it comes in the shape of a political football. It cannot. Community doers know that ignoring politics assures CDC trouble. But making politics a main agenda could destroy any CDC.

Given political realities, however, Bell of Pennsylvania was well advised to consider the delicacy of CDC formation. In North Philadelphia—or anywhere else—outside partners do not pick their way alone through competing community factions, unless they don't mind staggering back to headquarters carrying their heads in their hands.

Bell knew better, and their man, Chuck Powell, handled matters masterfully; he used partnership links to deal with the Memorandum's Paragraph III.

Responsible people at City Hall were fully aware of the importance of an East of Broad CDC. It could be helpful in articulating community 'how tos' and 'whats'; it could be a conduit through which partnership resources might flow; no less important, it could be a very useful heat shield.

There was no question where the East of Broad power sat. It sat with the two activists who, from the beginning, had led the strongest contingent against Temple and Bell. They were Paula Brown and Shirley Kitchen. These two women shared one very important insight that put them out in front of all other would-be group leaders: That a corporate investor in an inner-city community could be made a partner with that community in a focus on overall mutual growth.

"We were informed that that was an unrealistic concept," Shirley Kitchen said in our interview. "You didn't—you couldn't—hold a corporation responsible for participating in a community partnership. Even the city people said it was unrealistic. 'What's your leverage?' they asked us. We told them, 'Our land. Our bodies. We'll lay down on the building lot.' . . . Even some of our own people didn't go for this—they thought it was unrealistic."[9]

As the elected leader of the 29th Ward in North Philadelphia, Shirley Kitchen is politically astute. She and Paula Brown had long served together as ward committeepersons. They felt that the city, through late 1985 and early 1986, had tried to shape and control the East of Broad CDC board, to name a director of its own—and not necessarily one of the community's choosing.

The major city group working with Bell to help develop an East of Broad CDC was Dave Brenner's Department of Commerce through his deputy, Joe James. James assigned the task to Deputy Director of Commerce Elaine H. Black, a slender, vivacious, native Virginian in her thirties, with more than a decade of experience in Philadelphia community development.

"The mayor brought the Memorandum, the written agreement, to the Commerce Department and told us to help implement it," she said in our recent interview. "I got the job."[10]

Her job, what she in fact sees as the key local government role in *any* inner-city partnership, is to take the lead in promoting a clear definition of issues, and then to begin to work on solutions by harnessing private sector and institutional skills to community need.

"Networking, catalyst, whatever words fit," she said. "Our job is community understanding and coordination first. Here, for example, there was formal, lawyer-like language in the final Memorandum of Agreement that folks didn't really understand." So reachable goals had to be defined and agreed upon.

Working with Bell and the East of Broad group, Black had to help build trust as well as look for ways to develop program goals in order to get a new commu-

nity development corporation not only up, but running.

Once there is agreement on leadership structure and operational goals, community groups should be led to resources. The East of Broad people had Bell of Pennsylvania and the city. City officials like Black should be able to lead groups that need skills to others with skills (for example, private-sector lawyer volunteers). Officials like Black also know if scarce city resources are, in fact, available, and if there are state and federal funds around to be tapped as well. Still, individuals willing and able to work together toward shared goals are the basic program resource for communities.

"Putting people together," Black is convinced, "really isn't easy. But that is the name of the development game for folks in city government."

She believes that too little of the kind of focused coordination that went on with the city of Philadelphia, Bell of Pennsylvania, and the East of Broad leadership is actually promoted by branches of local government—in her own city and elsewhere. It appears that many systems, housing departments for example, seem not to like partnerships with community people. Community leaders can be difficult to work with, of course. Nevertheless, Black feels, "The real problem is that too much is all tied up with what the system sees as its personal turf."

That wasn't a tie-up here. Elaine Black is proud of the role her city played in helping form the CDC. In her view, another big reason why the Bell–North Philadelphia private sector–public sector partnership stands out has to do with the quality of the people who gave so much of themselves to make things work.

"In most cities," she says, "the best brains do the downtown work. The rest do inner core. Here, for once, it was different."[11]

Given the reality of several existing groups in the East of Broad Street area, notably Hispanic as well as black, it says much for Bell, Brown, Kitchen, Black, and their associates that a responsible CDC was put together as quickly and as effectively as it was. The perceptions of who favored whom, and who wanted exactly what, are no longer clear—and probably not even relevant.

Other partnership links, which included other community development–oriented human resource organizations, were also promoted by Bell and the city. Two of them were the Institute for the Study of Civic Values (ISCV) and one of its support groups, the Neighborhood Development Center (NDC).

ISCV is, in the broadest sense, a school for citizens. It provides classes, workshops, and mini-conferences in such areas as budgeting and proposal writing for nonprofit organizations, consumer credit, community work, and computer privacy issues. Its director, Jane Schull, a respected community educator, worked with Bell, the city, and the Neighborhood Development Center on the East of Broad CDC project. The NDC is an information clearinghouse and networker for community groups, and it also provides technical assistance to community-based organizations in Philadelphia in such areas as organizational development, fund raising, management, and board and staff development.

In December 1985, Bell, through Chuck Schalch and Chuck Powell, arranged with the Urban Coalition to fund a position for a person to work with the NDC. The purpose was to help put the East of Broad CDC together both internally with its programs and externally with community organization. The necessity for Bell's funding such a position was that while the nonprofit NDC mandate was broad, its budget was narrow and its staff too thin to allow one person to be assigned exclusively to one coordinating task. The reason for funding the prepaid position *through the Urban Coalition* was very sensible.

Bell could hardly fund the position of an East of Broad Community organizer directly. That would have left the company exposed to some very harsh elements. The Urban Coalition was more than a shield. It provided two other specific benefits. The first had to do with taxes. Monies put through this responsible group qualified Bell for special tax breaks through the Neighborhood Assistance Act. Specific corporate funds put into the CDC effort cost the corporation less than thirty cents on the dollar. But even more important was the issue of responsibility for the proper use of Bell's money. Whether it funded community development corporation activity for Bell through the umbrella group NDC, or, as it later did, by distributing funds to the CDC directly, the Urban Coalition itself remained responsible for auditing all expenditures and for ultimate accountability to Bell.[12]

The position of the NDC Community Coordinator for East of Broad CDC development was filled on December 16, 1985, and the contract was forwarded to the Urban Coalition for processing.[13] This new coordinator had the great advantage of NDC oversight and expertise being available to him as he provided technical assistance to East of Broad operations. The new coordinator was a black community activist named William Brown.

Brown, who was supported for the position by Councilman Street, had been a community organizer for the Black Panthers. He knew North Philadelphia well, had recruited local people in the past for construction jobs, and, overall, was clearly qualified for the NDC job. Nevertheless, it happens that he was married at the time to Paula Brown (now Paula Brown Taylor). William Brown's appointment, his qualifications notwithstanding, was related in part to political control issues. It would be hard to argue against that.

In any event, the East of Broad Community Development Corporation was organized and incorporated formally on March 21, 1986. Its mission was, in its own words:

To aid community residents through job training, employment counseling and placement and to participate in the improvement and stabilization of the East of Broad area through the initiation of housing, social services programs, educational scholarships, economic and business development projects, and to reinforce cultural awareness throughout the community.[14]

With offices on North Broad Street, its executive director was Paula Brown Taylor; its board chairperson, Shirley Kitchen. These were the two who had carried the fight to Temple and Bell, and who had, in the waning days of 1985 and the first months of 1986, set up meetings and working groups with many community organizations on gentrification, taxes, unemployment, crime, education, and similar issues to be faced by a new CDC. And they were the two who had argued, almost alone, that corporations should and *could* be pressed into productive community partnerships. Now, they had some learning to do and some training to absorb before the Memorandum of Agreement could result in substantive benefits for the community.

The East of Broad CDC became operational in July 1986, by means of a $75,000 grant from Bell of Pennsylvania, placed with the Philadelphia Urban Coalition. Bell's pledge was to give this amount for four years through June 1990.[15] The city of Philadelphia pledged to do the same, and Chuck Schalch and Chuck Powell of Bell have kept on the backs of city personnel to see that the funds—some of which must come through federal grants—are, in fact, released.

Benefaction and bribery look much the same when the only participant commitment is to an open purse. Therefore, in a partnership truly dedicated to helping a community make itself whole, *every* partner must

also become directly involved in the working process of growth.

By 1987, Bell of Pennsylvania's North Philadelphia contributions had clearly gone well beyond dollars and cents. Chuck Schalch's provision of a decent budget to supplement his district manager Chuck Powell's effort was certainly important. But equally important was the networking and other community organization work which kept Powell in close contact with community planners and with people on the street. A good example of giving both personal and policy direction partnership support—as well as funds—is to be found in the Norris Homes program.

The Norris Homes, with a total population of approximately three thousand people and located at the northeast corner of the Temple campus, is one member of an overall Philadelphia public housing project group in which adult residents, at year-end 1985, were eighty-five percent unemployed. The Bell/Temple/City joint effort that resulted in the Norris Homes Career Mobility Center created, in fact, the first job preparation program located at any such housing project in the city.[16]

In 1986, the Center, located behind the Bell PCC and next to Temple's Gladfelter Hall, had serviced or was continuing to service 139 participants. Thirty-two of them became employed full-time, earning money and no longer receiving welfare. The program also produced three matriculated college students. It is important to remember that this Center serves people usually defined as "hard-core unemployed"—in other words, people who have enormous problems beyond joblessness, and who require "substantial and sensitive support and follow up."[17] Most of what they require, to begin with, is hope.

Betty Jackson understands that. A stocky, determined black woman in her forties, Jackson moved into the Norris Homes complex in 1976. She had five children, then ages eleven, ten, nine, seven, and five.

Public housing east of Broad Street. (Nona Short)

Corner, North Philadelphia. (Nona Short)

Temple University, North Philadelphia. (Nona Short)

North Philadelphia intersection. (Nona Short)

Children playing, North Philadelphia. (Nona Short)

Bell of Pennsylvania Computer Center. (Nona Short)

Three lively wall paintings, North Philadelphia. (Nona Short)

Wall painting, North Philadelphia. (Nona Short)

Divorced and on welfare, she worked hard to keep them straight, making them study and remain in school. But for several years she was not involved in any way in her community.

"I was approached to come to a community meeting in the Homes here," she recalled, "maybe five years or so after I moved in. Well, I went after a while and there were some of us trying to make things better for folks at Norris Homes. But we didn't have any real voice to get things done."[18]

For a couple of years she attended meetings of the Norris Homes Tenant Council, which was under the leadership of Diane Gass. But the council simply did not have the means to accomplish anything substantial for the tenants.

"Change came," Betty Jackson makes clear, "when Bell came into our community."

It wasn't just the computer center. Not that concept alone. It was good but Bell gave us more. They gave us new ideas too. Chuck Powell came here to talk with community folks. And Sy Rosenthal from Temple. And they talked about putting a center here. They talked with us. I mean, here's what we want to do, here's why, and what do you folks think? Diane Gass liked the idea of training for careers. I was secretary of the Tenant Council then and I liked it, too. And that center really came.

The first class began in late 1985, but Betty Jackson did not enroll in it.

"It was hard to get a lot of people involved in the program at first," she admits.

Why were so few attracted to it?

"Too many satisfied to stay on welfare."

But that isn't why Jackson stayed out: "I've always wanted to move ahead. I just didn't go at first."

Some stayed away because they couldn't read or write and were too ashamed to reveal that. But that wasn't Betty Jackson's problem either.

"I just didn't go," she says haltingly, when pressed, "because I wasn't sure it would work *for me.*"

It appears that one could press one's children to stay clean and in school, and one could be involved in the attempt to improve one's community. But those were ongoing long-term struggles where the game was played out one day at a time with no immediate positive, substantial result expected by anyone. It would take more than the mere establishment of a center to bring Betty Jackson to the belief that she could put herself on the line, in full view of her community, and hope to come out quickly as a winner.

But then the first Mobility Center class graduated and Betty saw others actually beginning to progress.

"I saw things they were doing—like taking tests for real jobs and all. . . . And I *wanted* to get off welfare. . . . So, maybe I could . . . So, I went in."

She finished with the second group in May 1986, and was employed by VISTA as a worker with the Neighborhood Adult Basic Education Program, mainly administering and scoring tests. She recalled:

About six months after I started working, Chuck Powell from Bell came over to the Tenant Council and brought us the idea that we should have a full-time, paid organizer here who could help get community programs going. We had a community center, but our only real program was the Bell-Temple one. And what we talked about with Bell and in our group were things like teen programs, drug programs, education, tutorial, things like that.

Betty Jackson applied for the job of Community Organizer for the Norris Homes, with salary to be paid through the Urban Coalition with funds supplied by Bell of Pennsylvania. She was hired in February 1987.

Less than two months later, construction of the corporate computer center in North Philadelphia would come to an end. But not the constructive in-

Berks Street scene. (Lewis Downey)

volvement of the community's ongoing partner, Bell, through whom Betty Jackson, working mother of five, would be embarked on a new beginning.

The total Bell/Temple Norris Homes effort was not limited to a structured program affording accessibility to a career-ladder path and growth-oriented occupations. In addition to its $30,000 per annum contribution to the operation of the Center itself, Bell also helped plan for, and contributed $33,000 to, the establishment of a contiguous Day Care Drop-in Unit to ease the parent and staff child-care burden that comes from the adults' participation in training and counseling sessions. [19]

Temple's Center for Social Policy and Community Development, which operated the highly visible, productive Norris Homes Center, had some ideas of its own regarding future plans. As expressed through its director, Sy Rosenthal, one major goal would be to further partnerships of public and private agencies that would focus on expanding the kind and amount of service rendered to the housing project. These specific partnerships would be called Task Forces on Service Concentration. Then Rosenthal would,

using Bell of Pennsylvania as a model, enlist the cooperation of other business and corporate leadership in providing expertise, materials, equipment and direct financial support to the Norris project . . . [a] Community Endowment Operation. [20]

Another crucial Temple Center focus for the future (which could have applications well beyond the area of the Norris Homes) suggested the development of

[a] mechanism for identifying, recruiting and utilizing the vast resources of this University which the faculty, staff, administration and Board of Trustees represent, and target this enormous potential energy to support the efforts of the Norris community to improve its own quality of life. This program could serve as a

model for a permanent Temple and Community-Action Team . . . [aimed at developing] housing, health, social service and educational skills . . . [and the] development of an integrated and effective employment system for the entire neighborhood.

Such initiatives, indeed, "would be greatly enhanced by the participation of members of the entire Temple family." [21]

In addition to activities connected to the Norris Homes, Bell of Pennsylvania by 1987 also contributed funds and expertise to a three-year program in scientific, that is, computer, literacy at the Dunbar and John Wanamaker Public Schools near its PCC; Bell also contributed to such community development groups as the National Temple community housing and economic development program and a key Hispanic agency, ASPIRA.

Paragraph IV of the Memorandum of Understanding refers to the creation of a scholarship fund to benefit worthy students residing in the community which "the City shall initiate and Bell of Pennsylvania shall cooperate to promote." That language is a bit obtuse, but Bell's response was not. With a donation of $50,000, it created the Camille Cosby Scholarship in Science at Temple—a commitment to science education for community high-school graduates of modest means. The first student recipient was named in June 1986, at a ceremony attended by Temple trustee and alumnus Bill Cosby. [22]

The East of Broad Community Development Corporation, calling upon the skills-training support of the Neighborhood Development Center and the financial assistance of Bell, had begun its own job-training program involving computers and computer skills, and had developed a block captains program, a "clean block" program, and homeowner workshops to develop resident care and upkeep of property skills. It also worked with other agencies on emergency food programs, employment counseling, and displacement services, and on a Graduate Equivalency Diploma program to upgrade the qualifications of East of Broad job applicants. In 1987, the East of Broad CDC sponsored the first North Philadelphia Community Planning Conference, bringing together representatives from all over North Philadelphia to review and edit the city's *North Philadelphia Plan*.[23]

All this was just a beginning, of course, for the CDC. Much remained to be done in 1987 and beyond as construction on the new corporate computer center drew to a close and formal opening ceremonies were set for April 29. Beyond community development tasks, a CDC relationship with Bell had to ripen, and one with Temple had yet to begin.

Bell of Pennsylvania, in addition to establishing links with the overall North Philadelphia community, pursued growth connections with its partner, Temple. Its computer center, it must be remembered, was supposed to be the first corporate occupant in a projected Temple High-Tech Park—a Park envisioned as the single largest spur to overall economic progress in North Philadelphia.

The Temple concept differs from that inherent in such undertakings as the University of Pennsylvania/Drexel University City Science Center. While not downplaying its many merits, some Temple people view that and similar operations as having, to a certain degree, a real estate enterprise focus. More to Temple's—and Bell's—liking is the New Haven high-tech park located in an economically depressed inner-city university community, and anchored, interestingly enough, by a New England Bell Telephone operations center. The New Haven surroundings are not the equivalent of the PCC in any substantial way; however, the similarities were sufficient for Bell of Penn-

sylvania's Schalch and Powell and Temple's Hilty to visit New Haven and to check out their ideas.[24]

The final written proposal for the Temple project, completed after consideration of a plethora of internal and external input was: *The Temple University Science and Technology Campus and Jobs Program*, printed and released in March 1987.[25] Temple is convinced that it possesses the unique capability to fuse basic and applied research into the economic development of its immediate surrounding communities, and the full region of southeast Pennsylvania as well—if the state, the city, and job-creating businesses cooperate.

Businesses coming into the Science and Technology Campus and Jobs Program (the STC) could be the recipients of some highly desirable technology transfers that could be translated into commercial project development, jobs, financial profit, and human growth. For example, Temple University owns and could license patents involving medicines and biological preparations, as well as others related to engineering, genetics, and even electrical sciences such as superconductivity.[26]

While the actual Science and Technology Center of the total STC would be the major focus for a university-business liaison, there would be a Small Business Incubator as well, and a specific Jobs Training Program. The Incubator site would be the Temple-refurbished Atlantic Terminal Building, which would provide centralized services (copier, telephone answering, clerical, and the like), managerial assistance, and access to planning resources—all to small-growth high-tech-oriented firms willing to locate in North Philadelphia. The Jobs Training Program component of the STC would be modeled on the Norris Homes Career Mobility Center created by Temple and Bell of Pennsylvania.[27]

Of course, all participants in the STC would have the added advantage of access to amenities of the university such as library and recreation facilities and cultural and sporting events.

Bell of Pennsylvania and the Ben Franklin Partnership Program contributed $20,000 a year, for two years, for developmental planning for the Small Business Incubator. Temple is not without experience in the small business area. Its existing Small Business Development Center, with help from Bell of Pennsylvania, has conducted courses for start-up, minority-owned firms in North Philadelphia.[28]

Temple had every right to be excited about the future of its Science and Technology Campus and Jobs Program as the construction of the first tenant's building was about to come to an end. The open issue, of course, was just how fast progress would come after the Bell computer center was dedicated.

As April 29 drew closer, Bell and Temple were also involved in cooperative programs apart from the PCC. Beginning in April 1986, Chuck Schalch's Task Force meetings were expanded to accommodate relevant Temple University personnel. The major task the combined group first addressed was to enchant the Bell disenchanted. Despite the initial efforts of CEOs Smith and Wetzel and follow-up by other top executives, enthusiasm on the part of existing ISO computer center staff for the North Philadelphia move was hardly very high. And it should be remembered that not only were people to be moved, but these same people also had to be relied on to migrate (transfer) computer applications efficiently.

Leading the enthusiasm-for-Temple team was Temple's top enthusiast, Liacouras's assistant Bonnie Squires. Squires gives more meaning than most to the concept of achievement through radiating nervous energy. Working out of an office that always looks as if it has just been hit by a tornado, she serves as editor of the *Temple Review*, Assistant Secretary of the Temple Board of Trustees, and general utility infielder and outfielder for the Peter Liacouras squad.

"I was concerned," she said once she managed to sit down, "about the Bell managers' trepidation about trekking up to North Philadelphia. So I got up a presentation for them in order to encourage *them* to encourage the Wayne and Schuylkill workers. What we did was produce a special *Guide to Temple University*." She also arranged for Bell memberships at the Temple Faculty Club, and for discount theater tickets and cut-rate tickets for sports events for Bell employees. Moreover, as part of her job to bring staffs together, Squires used Bell of Pennsylvania's PCC employees presentation kit, and a fine audiovisual presentation prepared by Judy Coe and Ed Parsons of Bell's ISO, to orient Temple officials. She flung ninety-six of them together to be sure they understood and appreciated the new Bell computer center. She also used her editorial position to publish pieces on Bell and the PCC in the *Temple Review*.

"The whole idea was to make the transition a positive experience and idea for *everybody* involved," she said. Knowing that "everybody" was meant literally, one couldn't help but marvel.

"Our Joint Task Force has completed phase one. Now we're in phase two. No more just knowing and accepting each other. We're undertaking productive work between us—and to the mutual advantage of both Bell and Temple. Bill Tash [then Acting Dean of Graduate Studies] and I have been to Bell to talk to Chuck Schalch, and who knows what research projects will come out of this."

She talked about some work going on in the State of Oregon, through its governor, where heavy industry apparently works with the legislature "as cheerleader" to encourage larger appropriations to higher education.

"A lot of energy can get created," she said energetically, "by the synergy between corporations and higher education."[29]

So far, she seems to be right. Apart from her list of future goals for the Temple/Bell affiliation, there are already solid accomplishments. On November 12, 1986, Bell presented a $1-million gift to Temple to establish a professional chair in telecommunications, aimed at attracting prominent scholars and strengthening Temple as a center for research and education in the field. Not incidentally, the donation also aimed at providing a wider potential executive talent pool for companies in the business—like Bell of Pennsylvania.[30]

The Joint Task Force worked on other issues in 1986 and 1987. In addition to discussions concerning the contemplated high-tech campus, one of the most important was PCC security. The final result here was that the entire Temple main campus security force was provided with special quarters in, and now works permanently out of, the Bell computer center building.

The Joint Task Force meeting of April 20, 1987, was unique, and not so much for substance. It was the last one the group was to have before the partnership dream went public: The Bell of Pennsylvania/Diamond State Telephone Philadelphia Computer Center, at 12th Street and Montgomery Avenue, was formally dedicated on April 29, 1987.

The governor of Pennsylvania and the mayor of Philadelphia were there,[31] as, of course, were the presidents of Temple and Bell, and a large contingent from the East of Broad community.[32]

Beyond the party-like appearance of the yellow-striped tent outside under which the convocation gathered, beyond the bright balloons, the jazz on the lawn, and the gentler sound of the woodwind trio upstairs inside the building, and certainly beyond the politicians' gleaming black cars, the fawning hangers-on and officious aides, and the rest of the politician/

reporter hustle, there was, in truth, a special air about this ribbon-cutting ceremony. The reason for that was explained clearly and succinctly in a subsequent community newspaper editorial:

Bell Telephone is a statewide corporation that . . . could have gone anywhere, but it chose Temple. More important than that, this multi-million dollar mega-corporation chose to build and invest in a Black community. What more powerful statement attesting to the goodness, faith and potential of a community could have been made about North Philadelphia? Bell put its money where its mouth is.[33]

And, it might have been added, Bell acted with a tremendous amount of heart.

Peter Liacouras, in his formal remarks, referred to Bell's decision to locate where it did as "the single most important decision" in North Philadelphia's history, reversing a generation of exodus by private industry. Mayor Goode, who appeared to be truly moved, lauded Gil Wetzel, and Governor Casey was sincerely enthusiastic about this Bell investment being "a turn to the future," a corporate investment that for once would "leave no one behind."

Upstairs, inside the building following the formal ceremonies, a large crowd from Bell, Temple, and the community shared lunch and bewildering tours of the fantastic facility. Tour guides were patient and undoubtedly knew what they were talking about; however, all those computers, huge, medium, and small, and consoles and tapes and cassettes and wires and raised floors and differing temperatures were, together, a bit too much to absorb. Most tours ended with the tourists still mechanically ignorant.

But they were impressed, and not just by equipment. The feeling in the air was one of gratitude and hope—gratitude for acceptance on *everyone's* part, and hope that any partnership that could begin with a building like this might indeed bring economic reward and a new quality of life to *everyone* involved.

The Philadelphia *Inquirer* put it this way: "Governor Casey, who also spoke at the [Bell of Pennsylvania] dedication, is basing his state economic development program on the partnership concept. It *can* work."[34]

But it was Bell of Pennsylvania CEO Wetzel, in his formal remarks at the PCC dedication ceremony, who best put the reason for his company's entire North Philadelphia partnership thrust:

"There is only one way to predict the future," he said. "And that is to help shape it."[35]

Philadelphia Computer Center. Data Storage. (Nona Short)

4

THE

WORKING

MODEL

AND BEYOND

The Education Factor

R ich Masters is Bell of Pennsylvania district manager in charge of the Philadelphia Computer Center. He is responsible not just for providing service, but for relating sensitively to surrounding concerns, and for interface with Temple.

"In this job," he insists, "organization is everything." Intelligent, patient, and cooperative, Masters is one of those rare executives who seems to be able to locate immediately every piece of information related to every aspect of his work, whether it is sitting in a personal file, or a file in someone else's office, or even in a related employee's head.

In May 1987, he helped develop my understanding of how the PCC's hardware and software represented creative use of the latest in computer technology and advance design systems, and how everything worked to provide Bell of Pennsylvania/Diamond State with the most efficient and reliable data possible at de-escalating costs. In a February 1988 interview, he updated the status of his PCC applications migration from the Wayne Computer Center, completed in September 1987. That suburban facility was closed down just prior to October 1. Almost all Schuylkill applications had been migrated as well, and shutdown of that center had been set for August 1, 1988. All billing, corporate records, direct provision services (for example, time sharing); business office/client interactions; central repair services; special circuits; yellow pages—*all* the basic data supporting modern telephone company activities—are to be stored in this new home. The 250-car six-level parking garage next to the main PCC building (an additional $2.5 million investment) opened in August 1987. The garage was a matter of crucial importance to PCC employees concerned about convenience and security. By that time, all computer center security system elements, both human and mechanical, were also in full operation.[1]

With specific regard to community residents holding jobs inside the computer center, the results through 1988 were as good as might realistically have been imagined. Despite the fact that the total number of employees needed to staff the PCC had been revised downward to 173, there were eight positions filled by community residents. Three worked at management level positions (for example, as programmers), and five jobholders worked at non-management levels (for example, as computer tape handlers).[2]

This result does not come close to the twenty-five percent called for by the Memorandum of Understanding, of course. Bell of Pennsylvania has had problems as well hiring community residents in some of its other operations. While the PCC in one sense presents a special case—its personnel complement is in the process of being reduced—in another, both job placement situations demonstrate a common problem: the educational level, and consequent skills level, of too many community people is below that required to perform much company work competently, even at entry levels.[3]

North Philadelphia shares this problem in fundamental education with inner cities throughout the United States. It will not be solved by any single program or system, no matter how well funded. That is a reality which Bell of Pennsylvania, the North Philadelphia community, Temple University, and the city must grapple with if their ultimate partnership aim is to promote *long-term* inner-city regeneration. It is also an issue to be dealt with further in this book.

Bell as a partner did not turn idle once it formally opened the doors of its PCC. It continued to fund the Norris Homes Career Mobility Center, which, by the end of 1988, was taking on a different shape. By the terms of Paragraph II of the Memorandum of Understanding, "up to 300 Community residents, including Blacks, Hispanics and women [were to be trained] for the high-tech jobs as they became available in the Park."

The Temple "Park" had become the Temple Science and Technology Campus and Jobs Program, and it had not yet developed to the point where jobs existed for which people could be specifically trained. As a consequence, though the Career Mobility Center graduated more than two hundred people, most into clerical, factory, service care, retail, labor, and custodial jobs, it could no longer by the end of 1988 attract many more motivated trainees from the Norris Homes alone. Chuck Powell and Sy Rosenthal, representing Bell and Temple, have become engaged in developing a training program for youth from all of North Philadelphia who come out of high school, whether as graduates or dropouts. The central program will focus on helping them to take employment tests competently—a sort of SAT review for a different kind of admissions process.

Some youngsters will surely benefit from such a program. But to be successful, the North Philadelphia trainee, like the student at an SAT review course, has to bring to the experience a level of educational development sufficient to enable him or her to assimilate and use the training. This is a matter for serious concern in North Philadelphia, considering the low educational achievement of so much of the high school population.

In any event, this Bell/Temple effort, developed through helping the adult unemployed move into the job market, will call for help on the local Philadelphia Private Industry Council (PIC). There are some

630 PICs in the United States, created out of the Federal Job Training Partnership Act of 1982. These councils are quasi-governmental in nature and are usually made up of twenty-five members, fourteen from business and eleven from schools, unions, community-based organizations, employment services, and the like. PICs have their shortcomings, not the least of which is their often short-term business orientation. They have, however, some government funds and fine data access, and could certainly be a productive partner for a Temple-Bell training thrust toward youth, grown out of the Career Mobility Center experience.[4]

Paragraph IV of the Memorandum of Understanding called for the city to initiate, and Bell of Pennsylvania to cooperate, "in raising the sum of $2,000,000 for a developmental plan for that part of the [North Philadelphia] community east of Broad Street." A request for a proposal to deal with this issue did not produce an acceptable response. Bell and the city are working with a consultant—paid by Bell—on the establishment of a proper process for the development of such a complex and comprehensive plan.[5]

Bell of Pennsylvania's overall dollar commitment to various North Philadelphia community programs for the years 1988–1990 comes to more than $1 million. Two key recipient organizations are, of course, the Norris Homes Complex and the East of Broad Community Development Corporation.

The East of Broad CDC, in addition to activities undertaken in 1986 such as food distribution and Graduate Equivalency Diploma education, also began its own employment program, funded by Bell of Pennsylvania, in 1987. The CDC, working with the local PIC, which is an excellent provider of job availability data, utilizes a computerized assessment process focused on matching skills to available jobs.

Of course, the existence of skills is the key to everything. Here again, as with the question of job availability at Bell, the general low level of education and skills in the community might prevent a good number of matches.

During a December 1988 discussion of East of Broad CDC activities, Executive Director Paula Brown Taylor summed up her community's feelings about Bell of Pennsylvania this way:

Bell's done a lot for North Philadelphia. And it all started with their willingness to involve themselves with a community-based organization. The community here is very receptive to Bell. We know our people and let me tell you, they have very warm feelings toward Bell, and Bell has a really positive image. . . . Of course, they had to go through some pain initially, but they're benefiting now.[6]

And how about Temple?

Well, take the [1985] written agreement. Temple wouldn't touch it, right? They'd had the luxury of doing what they wanted in all of North Philadelphia and they saw our coalition as a hindrance to them. They were just plain arrogant.

Things have changed some, but when it comes to the doors of Temple, whether they're really open all the way and the welcome sign is out, well, we don't know that yet. You know, it isn't that Temple doesn't work with this small group or that one—just not with the community as such. The way Bell does.

Temple has undertaken an Exemplary Schools Program which is focused in large measure on getting parents involved with their children's schools. That program's history, in Paula Brown Taylor's eyes, is an example of what she sees as Temple's major problem:

Temple didn't go to the parents the first time around. They just decided what needs the program would see to. It was bad. The middle school district parents here in the community turned the program down. They wrote petitions to [Schools Superinten-dent] Connie Clayton saying Temple wanted to take their school over and close it. Now, this year, for the very first time, Temple has gone to parents in the com-munity, to see what they feel they need.

When Temple didn't sign the [1985] agreement, it was clear to all of us then that they weren't a complete partner. They had to come to see that they wouldn't benefit from that situation either.

Now Temple is trying to open up to the community more. I can't say we're on a trusting level, but we are on a level where we're talking to each other. I don't know how it will go yet, but we do have to search for common ground.

Temple has surely presented some evidence, at the highest level, of its willingness to participate in that search. Vice President for Administration Pat Swygert wrote in August 1988 to the East of Broad CDC leader-ship, pledging his office's willingness to explore com-munity development areas of mutual concern.[7]

As of March 1988, the East of Broad CDC allied it-self with two west of Broad community development centers in another kind of North Philadelphia part-nership. Their aim, in part, is to monitor the flow of all government development dollars into North Phila-delphia. Their goal is to have some input into area de-velopment processes, and it would be troublesome, surely, to obtain government funds for a North Phila-delphia project if this group presented substantial objections.

Paula Brown Taylor's position is clear. "We don't want to stop development. We just want the commu-nity involved as an equal partner. We want input and we want to help."

East of Broad CDC Executive Director Brown Tay-lor commuted from Philadelphia to New Hampshire College for eighteen months, and was recently awarded a masters degree in Community Economic

Development. She is enthusiastic about the future of commercial progress in her community.

The Girard Avenue strip is now being developed on three city-owned vacant lots, and we're planning for a new supermarket and other stores. We need them now so our community folks don't have to go elsewhere to shop. And we're talking with private developers, too, about modular town houses to increase private home ownership.[8]

Shirley Kitchen, the first East of Broad board chair-person, is surely high on the partnership idea. "We think that our partners have to be accountable to the community," she said in our interview.[9] When re-minded that the community itself was a partner to others she said,

Sure. We know the [Great Society] days are over. We don't want them anymore. We don't want things to be made easy. I agree with you about community people who confront and then run. That's negative. Only real change will make things work. We have to do things together.

When asked her opinion concerning community feeling for Bell of Pennsylvania, Kitchen smiled and said, "The whole community likes Bell. That com-puter center, not even one window is broken, right?"[10] As jocularly as those words were spoken, they were clearly a powerful symbolic statement about a very important symbol—one which already has had a pos-itive effect on the lives of many in the community.

With all of its positive movement, the East of Broad CDC is not without its problems. Problems have developed which boil down to this: What exactly is the authority and power and responsibility of the ex-ecutive director, and what exactly is the authority and power and responsibility of the CDC board? This cen-tral issue, currently being thrashed out in the midst of an ongoing East of Broad CDC growth process, is not an uncommon one in such community develop-ment efforts. What is uncommon here, however, is the degree of continuing involvement in the issue, as partners, of Bell of Pennsylvania and the city of Philadelphia.

Chuck Powell and Elaine Black have met, and plan to continue to meet, with Paula Brown Taylor and CDC board members who make up the feuding par-ties. The first 1989 meeting of the full board of direc-tors of the CDC, hosted by Bell of Pennsylvania at its Philadelphia headquarters, is a prime example of continuous full partnership involvement in ongoing community development. Powell and Black will con-tinue to insist that no individual personality is as im-portant as the CDC itself, which must be maintained in a healthy state as an organization responsive and responsible to the community.[11]

There has been very little progress to date in the de-velopment of Temple's Science and Technology Campus and Jobs Program (STC)—and a good deal of frustration.

The participation of the first STC tenant, Bell of Pennsylvania, was originally grounded on the pres-ence of a co-anchor, and on a new Southeast Penn-sylvania Transportation Authority (SEPTA) commuter train station stop. By the end of 1988, neither of these requirements had come to fruition.

It is true that the Philadelphia Gas Works con-structed a new $29-million executive office building close by the Bell computer center and the Temple campus; however, that is hardly the Macy's to Bell's Bloomingdale's. The commercial development and jobs potential are not the same. While PGW has signed an agreement of its own with the East of Broad CDC, and has provided funds for one feasibility study undertaken by the CDC, it has as yet done nothing sig-nificant or innovative in funding or developing com-munity programs, nor has it pursued strong commu-

nity ties in the manner of Bell's ties with the Norris Homes.

As for the delay in the construction of the new SEPTA station, there is a faint taste of disgrace about that political morsel. With a total cost, even today, of less than $10 million for the essential relocation to 10th and Berks, and with the city of Philadelphia put-ting its share of the funds into its capital budget each year, the question mark is the state of Pennsylvania. It may be true that there is much on the SEPTA demand list. But when the low cost and the need to provide a decent transportation site for business committed to putting investment dollars and jobs into North Phila-delphia are put together, one cannot help but con-clude that something is amiss here. The first thing that comes to mind is that inner-city Philadelphia, read minorities, sits far too low on any sensible and ethical state legislature priority list.

It can only be hoped that government at every level, as well as private industry, can be brought soon, by the Bell of Pennsylvania example, to see the mu-tual advantage of resource commitment to such a Sci-ence and Technology Campus and Jobs Program as Temple has delivered. For a commitment here can surely result in both profits *and* human growth.

Just how much of that human growth will take place for North Philadelphians, however, depends as much on positive development of the educational process in the community as it does on the develop-ment of the Temple STC. The Jobs Program can and should help train local people out of the primary- and secondary-school loop to fill some high-tech posi-tions. But training programs alone will never fulfill the task of revitalizing North Philadelphia in the long term. That accomplishment depends on the commu-nity's ability to relate far better than it has thus far to the education of its youth. The community must help to produce young people *able* to become skilled workers and even entrepreneurs. The alternative is a community resigned to the role of recipient of a bit of the earnings which trickle down from others; a community from which those relatively few youngsters who realize their full potential on their own will flee just as fast as they can.

Human growth has been Betty Jackson's main concern for a very long time, both in her own immediate family and in her broader community.

From early 1987 through 1988, with no end in sight, her efforts have remained concentrated on her Bell of Pennsylvania–inspired, and funded, job of Norris Homes Community Organizer. In that position, she helps conceive programs she'd like to see put into effect for the people in her Norris Homes community. When Jackson feels she has one that she'd like to move ahead on, she takes it to her immediate superior, Diane Gass, for approval, and then she begins to coordinate.

Community organizer Jackson has begun a substance abuse and teenage pregnancy program, an adult literacy program (conducted by the Mayor's Commission on Literacy), and several food programs, some of which involve small consumer payments and others where food is distributed free. One program in which she took special pride—now discontinued for lack of funds—was the Black Family Discussion Series, sponsored by the Mini-University connected with the Reverend Leon Sullivan's Zion Baptist Church. Films were shown, such as *Native Son*, and they were followed by very lively discussions.

Betty Jackson says,

I've got two different feelings about the future here at Norris Homes. I do see us moving ahead. We're doing things now in our community. But if we don't do something more about drugs, I can see the community here around us deteriorating. I see mothers who are users and their children being neglected.

I'm proud of Norris. Things aren't out of hand yet with the drugs. We've still got things under control, no shootings or such as that, but there are worries.

This North Philadelphia mother of five feels there is a close connection between education and the survival and growth of children in the presence of drugs and early pregnancy.

"Education!" Jackson says with conviction. "Education is what it's all about. And it starts with parents, with the home. My kids aren't real problems, but if I hadn't stayed on them, I know they wouldn't have stayed on through school."

It isn't that her children could completely avoid serious problem areas. Betty Jackson's daughter became pregnant in high school. But she did not drop out.

"If young people get pregnant, you stay with them. Parents have to because education's so important. It's what they have to have or else, well, just *forget* it!"[12]

As she spoke, it became clear that education for Jackson translated into a good job and a decent, responsible human existence—one in which there would be a good chance of avoiding illicit drugs and the kind of pregnancy which doesn't begin a new process of human growth, but rather ends such a process entirely. If effective education is not to be had in Jackson's community, either because it is unavailable to the community's youth, or because when it is available they refuse to involve themselves in it—or both—then the Bell of Pennsylvania partnership group has a top priority problem to address.

Bell and Temple have not completely overlooked the education issue. A telephone company–sponsored program, "Be the Best, Expect the Best," put in place in North Philadelphia's John Wanamaker Junior High and the Dunbar Elementary School, concentrates on the formulation of goals by the various school constituencies. Administrators, teachers, parents, and students work together after trying to set priorities for institutional progress within their own individual groups. Temple, in addition to its Exemplary Schools Program, pursues other connections with the local school system, such as helping some teachers to sharpen particular skills.[13]

But a close examination of the present disastrous state of primary and secondary education in North Philadelphia makes it clear that much more focused, innovative, and expanded efforts in education are required of this partnership and others if long-lasting community revitalization is to take place.

Public schools in North Philadelphia currently have the highest truancy, dropout, retention in grade, and absenteeism rates in the entire city system. They have the lowest standardized reading test scores as well. Edison High School in North Philadelphia has annually recorded the highest dropout rate of any high school in the system.[14] To all this must be added the general educational level to be found outside the schools: In the West Poplar, Temple Area, and Ludlow neighborhoods near the university, seventy percent of all adults twenty-five years of age or older have never completed high school.[15]

The Bell of Pennsylvania/Temple University/Community/City partnership has done much in and for North Philadelphia. The alliance has built a marvelous base upon which a revitalized inner city might arise. It does not belittle the partnership's many accomplishments to point out that most have been concentrated outside the primary and secondary schools, and to suggest that there can and should be a more substantial effort put forth in the area of innovative education.

The precipitating factor in the formation of this Philadelphia partnership was Bell of Pennsylvania's $125-million investment in an impoverished community. But if the PCC building is a symbol of faith in the future of the minority community in which it stands, it is also a grim reminder of the fact that if that community's capacity for dealing with the demands of technological change and for the rapid absorption and utilization of ever-increasing amounts of information is not vastly improved, it doesn't have a future.

Improving high-tech-information-age capacities does depend, to a small degree, on helping those currently in the working population who are capable to develop special skills. However, to a large degree, a fully capable North Philadelphia population for the future depends upon delivery now of effective education to the young.

Perhaps the clearest expression of the difficulties faced by poorly educated youth in or out of North Philadelphia, relative to their ever getting into a decent job opportunity, is this statement from R. E. Heckert, chairman of E. I. du Pont de Nemours and Company:

We do not employ people who do not have the basic skills because they are not able to benefit from the training programs we offer, and they are dangerous to themselves and to others in the workplace. . . . There is a limit to how far back we can and should go in training workers. Teaching reading, writing and arithmetic on a large scale is not our role, and neither is the teaching of values.[16]

It is neither possible to comprehend the true nature of the education problem east and west of Broad Street, nor to begin to relate successfully to innovative approaches available to deal with it, without arriving at some understanding of its national extent. The "why" and the "what" of a major North Philadelphia effort has to be linked to the full realization that this particular inner city reflects a much greater education problem existing throughout the United States.

To begin with, there are the dropouts.

North Philadelphia contributes to a total of some seven hundred thousand to one million young people leaving the nation's high schools each year without graduating.[17] While the exact number is not firm, there is firm agreement on the problem dropouts present: "Most of them will be deficient in basic skills, marginally literate, and virtually unemployable."[18]

Not all who do remain in school end up much better off: "Another 700,000 [young people] will merely mark time in school and receive their diplomas but will be as deficient in meaningful skills and work habits as most dropouts."[19]

The source for the two previous quotes is not a well-known "liberal" publication beating the drum for taxpayer dollars to throw at yet another social problem. The quotes originated in an eighty-five-page statement issued by a policy group representing the Committee for Economic Development, an independent research and development organization made up of more than two hundred business executives and educators. Among its members at the time the statement was approved and released were the chief executive officers of such corporations as General Motors, General Foods, Eli Lilly, Primerica, Honeywell, and TRW. Their statement was not a mere concession to the public in the direction of general corporate social responsibility. American business executives are deeply concerned about their own and their nation's competitiveness in the world in the face of so many young people clearly unprepared to handle meaningful jobs.

They have every reason to be. The United States Office of Education estimates that we already have 17 to 21 million functional illiterates in the marketplace, and the most recent estimates of the cost to U.S. business of productivity losses caused by poorly educated workers is $25 billion a year.[20]

There is also concern for the future. Some of the dropouts and otherwise poorly prepared will enter felonious enterprises such as the illicit drug trade. Their activity will promote further intellectual decay. Exact data on young pushers and users would be hard to come by, of course. But there *is* data confirming the fact that dropouts in general perpetuate a vicious cycle: dropping out is linked to poverty, and consequent poverty to further dropping out.

During 1982–1983, in families in which both parents were high school graduates, only 7 per cent of the children were poor. If only one parent was a high school graduate, 20 percent of the children were poor. And where neither of the parents was a high school graduate, 39 per cent of the children were poor.[21]

Yet despite the fact that the majority of dropouts are minority non-whites,[22]

when poverty rates are controlled for, black and white drop-out rates are essentially identical. Regardless of race, youths from poor families are three to four times more likely to drop out of school than those from more affluent households.[23]

Stated in terms of a family's ability to avoid poverty we see that . . . when the family is headed by a single mother with limited education, the incidence of poverty increases dramatically, reaching 81 to 92 per cent depending on her age.[24]

The relationship of this disturbing national data to the Bell of Pennsylvania partnership locale is painfully apparent, as is the fact that it suggests one focus for a priority educational thrust. For in some North Philadelphia neighborhoods, sixty-one to seventy-six percent of all households are headed by single mothers with limited education.[25]

There are two concerns posed by the fact that some 1.5 million American children, the majority of whom are minority poor, are doomed each year to the severe consequences of functional illiteracy. The first is moral: that in our affluent society, most of these youngsters will not have the opportunity to grow as human beings, to enjoy the kind of human connections at work and at leisure that result in respect for

Berks Street—playground. (Lewis Downey)

oneself and respect for others, that result in feelings of accomplishment and pride, in at least a modicum of material rewards, and in nourishing interdependencies. Most will not have, in sum, anyplace to be somebody.

The second concern does not have to be related to ethics—it stands on its own as a major catastrophe. That concern is economic. An internationally respected professor of economics puts it this way:

But perhaps [our] greatest omission . . . has been the lack of investment in the most socially and economically productive capital: human beings. . . . A bigger industrial plan, a sane trade policy and a stable social and political environment for economic calculations . . . all contribute to better per capita growth. But how can [any] economic sector successfully modernize if there is so vast an insufficiency of investment in human capital?

The reference here is not to the United States. The professor is commenting on his developing nation, Mexico.[26] We Americans may use the term "developed nation" when we refer to ourselves, but we surely share similar human capital problems. In the United States today,

The labor pool of younger workers who historically fill entry-level jobs is declining in both number and quality, for reasons ranging from the demographic to the social, while the jobs waiting for them require even more knowledge and skill.[27]

David Kearns, chairman of Xerox Corporation, says, "Education is a bigger factor in productivity growth [rates] than increased capital, economies of scale or better allocation of resources."[28]

A spate of articles in the popular and business press also attests to the huge problem U.S. industry faces, of finding enough young adults capable of operating state-of-the-art equipment, and in dealing with the shortage of educated workers. The problem is, in fact, inextricably linked to America's competitive future in the world.

What U.S. companies increasingly will get is women, minorities and immigrants whose educational opportunities have traditionally been limited. For the rest of the century, these groups will make up 80 per cent of new workers.[29]

What we have here, to quote University of Maryland economist F. Levy, is "a blueprint for national decline."[30] A national decline, it would seem, in which educational weakness, less competitiveness in world markets, and the creation of a permanent underclass in inner-city areas such as North Philadelphia could all be linked in a particular vicious cycle.[31]

One way to break that cycle, in North Philadelphia and elsewhere in America's cities, is to provide an educational process that prepares many graduating high school students for productive futures as workers and as good citizens in an age of rapid change. But another way has to be to ready some for higher education, unless we choose to deliver the message that going to college is not a game inner-city kids should even dream of playing.

An editorial in a major American newspaper recently asked of young people like those who make up a major portion of North Philadelphia's poor: "Do [they] drop out because they can't afford college, or because they simply can't imagine it?"[32]

If America can't imagine it, the vicious cycle is likely to continue, fed in locales such as North Philadelphia, and to grow so large as to push us out of our current position as the major economic and democratic power in the world.

The question surely must be asked here whether higher education in the United States is up to the future needs of our inner cities and our nation.

At the college undergraduate level, bad news confronts all blue-collar families. Enrollment of their children, as a percentage of the total, dropped by twenty percent in the 1980 to 1986 period. Between 1976 and 1985, black and Hispanic enrollment fell even more, by approximately twenty-five percent. [33]

There are problems at the graduate level as well, where the nation must depend in substantial measure on Ph.D.'s for excellence in areas such as mathematics, computer science, physics, astronomy, chemistry, engineering, genetics, and biology. The total number of Ph.D.'s awarded seems in general to be declining. [34] Certainly, the percentage of foreigners who obtain Ph.D.'s from U.S. universities is rising relative to American citizens. This is particularly true in the sciences. In 1986, for example, foreigners earned fifty percent of the total number of doctorates awarded in computer engineering. [35]

There is nothing sinister about the mere fact that so many foreigners come to America to pursue excellence at its source. Many will stay and contribute to progress in the nation. But excessive reliance on foreigners to make up for native shortfalls, with our education as with our debt, might well prove a long-term folly. The question of why fewer Americans are pursuing graduate education may well be related to the urge to make as much money as possible right away. Some fields, such as engineering, are suffering from industrial short-term myopia. Many of America's high-technology giants are reducing production and professional staffs in order to show a better profit *now*. This approach, combined with demographic and social trends that result in less and less serious educational preparation, is setting America up for a fall. The Commission on Professionals in Science and Technology predicts that by the middle of the next decade there will not be enough engineers of any age to design solutions to our most pressing technical problems. Says the Commission's executive director, "The situation could undermine both our own national security and our industrial competitiveness." [36]

Given our nation's crucial needs for educated professionals, one can appreciate the powerful public service messages prepared by the Advertising Council for the United Negro College Fund: A mind *is* a terrible thing to waste. [37] And the nation can no longer morally or economically afford such waste.

The graduate-level situation with regard to minorities in America is grave. Of some 31,700 doctorates awarded in all fields in the United States in 1986, less than three percent went to black Americans, two percent to Hispanic Americans, and three-tenths of one percent to Native Americans. Six blacks received Ph.D.'s in some area of mathematics, one in the computer sciences, twenty-four in engineering (but none in computer engineering), none in biophysics or architecture, a total of eight in the fourteen subspecialties of physics and astronomy, a total of five in the twenty subspecialties falling under "teaching fields," and, perhaps saddest of all, a total of eighty Ph.D.'s out of the 3,461 awarded in the eighteen categories classified as "the humanities." [38] What we must conclude from this data is that from educational floor to educational ceiling, we face the reality of economic and general developmental stagnation, both for the inner cities' already disadvantaged and for the nation as a whole.

The reasons for this primary, secondary, and higher education disaster for minorities are complex. They begin before birth for many children as poor as those in North Philadelphia. Such children are born to mothers without the benefits of prenatal care and they then experience continued poor nutrition, lack of immunization, and the thousand other ills the infant in poverty is heir to. [39] The Committee for Economic Development has detailed its concerns about the need to focus on the child from birth to age five if full progress is to be made regarding America's education problems.[40]

Then there is the school system itself. No one can deny the need for basic school restructuring. Still it could be argued that, in part, public school systems throughout the country are burdened with an outside load.

Ours is, after all, an adult society that refuses to take sufficient responsibility for so much poverty in the midst of plenty. We refuse as a group and individually to maintain a set of personal standards sufficiently high to motivate our children properly. We refuse to demand quality performance from ourselves, from our professionals in every field, and from our elected leaders. We tolerate ethical transgressions and misdemeanors and felonies in public and private life that, sometimes directly and sometimes subtly, pervert our children's outlook on how life should be lived. And we have so capitulated to materialism that we have disassociated the word "moral" from the word "value" and substituted for it the word "product." And then we wonder why our children have so much difficulty dealing with self-worth.

Public schools indeed have a heavy load to shed before getting down to the teaching and learning business. It does not excuse the public school system's failures to call attention to the fact that if education is to improve we must deal with the personal, as well as the public school, need for reform.

Related to personal reform are those problems presented by a failure of focus and will on the part of too many of the disadvantaged themselves. It is easy to push aside ridiculous arguments that it is moral and just that people with college degrees make more money than those who don't, since those who don't have nobody to blame but themselves.[41] But it is not so easy to absolve people of *all* responsibility for educational deprivation simply because they are poor, even in North Philadelphia. Dr. Clifford R. Wharton

stated the concern here rather well in his plenary address to the National Urban League Conference in 1986. After referring to the reality of societal neglect and the persistence of discrimination, Dr. Wharton went on to say that these reasons were

only partially adequate to explain skyrocketing drop-out rates and the erosion of Black gains in higher education. And [they are] unsatisfying because [they] raise the further question of why, two or three generations ago, Blacks somehow managed to advance educational goals even though the deck was stacked even more formidably against them. . . . Are persistent poverty and persistent discrimination obstacles to learning? Of course they are. Do delinquency, broken homes, alcohol and drugs, street culture, shoddy career counselling, youth unemployment, teenage pregnancy and all the other enduring pathologies of disenfranchisement sit at the bottom of some of today's drop-out crisis and eroding college participation rates? No doubt about it.

But are they the root of the entire problem?

[There is a challenge here to face] arising not altogether from discrimination, but at least in part from changes in the psychology and value system of the black community itself.

Dr. Wharton strongly suggests that positive self-images, aspiration, and achievement must be internalized by minorities through strengthening the family structure, and, overall, from within its own communities. After pointing out the remarkable success of blacks in the field of athletics, and the fact that such success is related to the willingness to work long and grueling hours of practice to achieve success, Dr. Wharton asks: "Where is our comparable intellectual competitiveness, our 'intellectual work ethic'?"[42]

Dr. Wharton's focus on community responsibility for effecting change is important for the Bell of Pennsylvania partnership to keep in mind as it seeks to expand its activities into the area of helping schools reach beyond traditional educational boundaries—which is, of course, what must be done in order to further the long term revitalization of North Philadelphia.

A productive initial partnership task would be to review some available examples of innovative programs dealing with specific problems currently faced both east and west of Broad Street.

Two programs developed by the Manpower Demonstration Research Corporation (MDRC) address the teenage pregnancy and female-headed family problems. New Chance prepares low-income single mothers, ages seventeen to twenty-one, for gainful employment in an intensive four-days-a-week, eighteen-month program. A major New Chance premise is that young women of working age are most likely to delay future pregnancies if they know they are sufficiently trained to succeed financially in the job market. The Community Woman component of MDRC's Project Redirection provides young pregnant women with mentors who help them to believe that if they work at it, they still *can* be somebody of value. The mentors, older women from their communities who have raised children and managed households successfully, provide not only emotional support, but instruction and problem solving as well.[43]

A particularly promising business education partnership was initiated in Boston several years ago. The focus was on mutual agreements—a "compact"—whereby schools would work to improve the quality of education, and businesses would work to give hiring priority to graduates of the schools. Each group in the partnership would have to specify clear goals in the compact, and there were many. The Boston School Department would, for example, improve daily attendance levels and math and reading competencies as well; the Boston business community would recruit firms which would pledge to give priority hiring status

to Boston high school graduates; local colleges would expand counseling to increase college enrollments, and the local Private Industry Council would coordinate with private businesses to provide career counseling in the city high schools. In each case, exact numbers and percentages were spelled out as goals.

Test scores, job hires, college enrollments, and overall school attendance are up consistently in Boston. However, although the overall dropout rate in the high schools is down, the fourth-year dropout rate is up. The compact partners are redoubling their efforts here.[44]

The State of California, building on Boston's experience, established a California Compact Program in 1988. State-level coordinators, made up of the California Departments of Education and of Employment Development, together with the state Business Roundtable and Chamber of Commerce, and the Employment and Training Administration of the U.S. Department of Labor, are pressing local communities to develop local compacts. But although goals and priorities will be set at local levels to meet local needs, each compact aims toward the same final goal: To assure

that every student graduating from California High Schools who meets the grade, discipline, attendance and instructional standards outlined by school and business officials in the local community will be guaranteed priority hiring status for jobs, or financial assistance needed to attend postsecondary education.[45]

The Cleveland Initiative for Education, also begun in 1988, is the first partnership of business, civic, ethnic, and religious leaders to offer scholarships to every child in a major city school system who chooses to go on to college. The Initiative also sponsors a "school-to-work-transition" program which guarantees priority hiring status for full-time entry-level jobs to those students choosing to go to work immediately.[46] The

Cleveland partners are so proud of their program that they actually advertise it commercially in such publications as the *Wall Street Journal* to attract new businesses into a city where the school system will provide them with a properly educated and motivated work pool.[47]

Counseling programs aimed at minority students who have traditionally not considered college are on the rise. By providing innovative counseling early, even in junior high, to poor and minority youth *and their parents*, such programs have been able to motivate large numbers of young people to go on with their education. Franklin High School in Los Angeles concentrates on such counseling and sends eighty percent of its largely Chicano student body into college.[48]

Many other unusual programs have been written about, and developers and operators of these programs are usually available for discussion. These efforts may be aimed at middle schools, or at accountability in post-secondary education, or at mentoring and peer-group counseling. But the bottom line for all such programs is that they must motivate the minority student to excel. They must nurture the student's capacity for intellectual growth that has been allowed to wither for too long.

The Bell of Pennsylvania partnership has much in the way of resources to call upon in dealing with the educational aspect of North Philadelphia revitalization.

The city can be utilized to coordinate various aspects of service delivery. Guidance, educational programs, financial and job training and support services, for example, demand the kind of putting-people-and-resources-together skills that such people as Elaine Black have to offer.

Temple University is a comprehensive teaching and research institution of high caliber, and is utterly competent to deal with innovative approaches to local education concerns. The basic problem seems to be that there has thus far been a lack of joint focus on the part of Temple and the community. While the Exemplary Schools program seems to be proceeding now, the priority educational concerns to be faced in North Philadelphia, and Temple's proper, most effective role as a community partner are issues remaining to be resolved with the community and with its partner, Bell.

Bell can certainly play a major role in areas apart from finance. It can help determine priorities and program directions, and to press the business community to understand and participate in finding solutions to educational concerns, from dropouts to jobs to encouraging youngsters to go on to college.

And Bell of Pennsylvania has to help light a fire under the remaining partner, the community. The East of Broad CDC, the Norris Homes Tenant Council and other community groups who respect and trust Bell should be pressed to discuss an educational thrust with as much fervor as they did the initial thrust to build the computer center. Community meetings might serve, for example, to help familiarize people with parent-community involvement efforts already undertaken elsewhere. One example is the Comer Process which has actually resocialized inner-city schools in New Haven through the use of management and governance, and mental health teams and *active parent participation*.[49]

Parents are the key, but parents are not enough. The entire community should be drawn in to accepting responsibility for preparing their youth for productive jobs and good citizenship. Economist Lester Thurow wrote:

I am willing to pay for, indeed insist upon, the education of my neighbor's children not because I am generous, but because I cannot afford to live with them uneducated.[50]

North Philadelphia can afford it even less.

I certainly do not suggest here that the community or the university "take over" the schools. What is suggested is that the community put itself on the line for educational development with at least as much enthusiasm as it showed for general partnership development back in 1985. The North Philadelphia community as a partner must accept equal responsibility with Bell, Temple, and the city for assuring the intellectual advancement of its youth. The job cannot be left to a program they have no part in at all.

This is not to say that better schools and better adjunct programs *cannot*, alone, rescue a student from an unconcerned community; most often they simply *don't*. There is no substitute for a community attitude, forcefully expressed, that says in effect: there may be much to do here, but the full development of your young minds is our priority task. Not one of you is going to be wasted, and we're *all* going to tend to that.

My own past experience in planning and administering drug abuse treatment, intervention, and prevention programs, over a period of thirteen years, has brought me to believe that when young people are the object of positive adult attention and concern; when they are made to believe that if they buckle down to it, there'll be help and plaudits forthcoming from parents and neighbors; when they feel that they are *valued* in their community—when they are, in other words, convinced that *there is a place for them to be somebody*—they will not make good customers for the scum pushing dope on their streets.

It cannot be denied that the Bell of Pennsylvania–Philadelphia partnership faces a daunting task in the thorough revitalization of the inner city. But it is in the right town, after all. It was another Philadelphia partnership facing an even tougher task that brought about the first true government of the people, by the people, and for the people ever established on this earth.

But there are so many problems, a cynic might argue. With all the good will in the world, it will take too long to solve them.

The story is told of a wise old man who retired to a warm climate. He asked his gardener to plant a certain tree whose lush foliage he much admired. Sadly, his gardener informed him that a tree as magnificent as that took two hundred years to reach full maturity.

"Then we have no time to lose," the wise old man replied. "We have to plant it today."

APPENDIX

ONE

HOW

DO

COMPUTERS

ACTUALLY

WORK?

Most people *don't* know how computers work. This is unfortunate because, lacking such understanding, it is difficult to appreciate fully the true nature of the tasks and accomplishments of a given group of computers, such as those hard at work in Bell of Pennsylvania's PCC.

The world's digital computers are all actually collections of switches. The switches are worked through electrical impulses that turn them on and off with absolutely incredible speed. Semiconductors, transistors, microchips, integrated circuits, microprocessors, and the like are all words describing physical parts and processes that use the element silicon—which is really smelted sand—to do the turning on and off. Silicon serves as the base for amplifying, conducting,

and processing electrical impulses. Miniaturization technology is also key because it allows these various computer parts and processes to do more amplifying, conducting, and processing, within an ever-shrinking amount of space. [1]

For example, miniaturization technology allows for 275,000 of these minute "gate switches" plus 1,000,000 other electrical components, such as electrical impulse conductors, to be placed on a single, quarter-inch-square silicon chip! [2] It is miniaturization and the speed at which these basic electrical impulses can be conducted that is at the heart of computer accomplishment. Although superconductivity holds out the future promise of transmission speeds beyond today's limitations,

111

the current top technology, which is incredible enough, is fiber optics: infrared light pushing electric impulses through glass fibers the thickness of a human hair.

Each electrical impulse sent to a switch turns it on. The absence of an electrical impulse leaves the switch off. While that doesn't seem to be an earthshaking accomplishment, the symbol power of the basic on-off one-two digital "binary code" allows these brief bursts of electricity to speak volumes.

What happens in computers is this: the electricity in the form of brief electric impulses rushed to the switch "instructs" it to be "on." Its absence is also an "instruction" to be "off." Using the binary system, which involves only two elements, 1 for yes and 0 for no, each switch when instructed to the "on" position is 1 (or yes); when instructed to remain in the "off" position, it is 0 (or no). Those are the basic digital computer symbols.

Such symbols would appear to present a serious quantity problem. We have coded them cleverly so that a certain combination of 1's and 0's equals a real letter (say B), and another combination equals a number larger than 1 (say 3,000). That is, we have taken the basic symbols and set up rules for combining them into understandable forms that make a "language."[3] Still, a very large number of simple 1's and 0's are required to get these symbols to represent sizable amounts of words and numbers. The volume of on-off instructions required to deal with the real-world information equivalent of a book, or numbers in a complex mathematical problem, is large indeed.

However, given the state of miniaturization technology and conduction technology, and our basic host, silicon, the quantity problem actually comes to nothing. Existing supercomputers can perform one billion such basic on-off instructions *per second*—an amount sufficient to cover all the information con-

tained in all the volumes making up the *Encyclopædia Britannica*. One *Britannica's* worth of instructions each *second!*[4]

It is true, of course, that mini-supercomputers can only perform some three to four hundred million such instructions per second (IPS), and large non-supercomputers only some tens of millions per second. Desktop computers are able to do even less; however, many desktop computer tasks require little more than several million instructions per second and anyway, more instructions per second are surely headed their way.[5]

Such bits of information (1-0, yes-no) are referred to as "bits," and so many "bits" as make up a single unit of "real" information, say a letter or a number, are referred to as "bytes." Bits and bytes, measures of the capacities of particular computers, must, of course, be thought of in more ways than just transmitted instructions per second.

A broader view requires a closer look at the actual functions of computers. All computers, whether super or hand-held, perform—through the medium of distinctly focused silicon chips—the very same five functions. These are:

1. *Input*
   They take in data.

2. *Storage*
   They have memory; they store the data received. They also store program instructions given to them on how to deal with received data; that is, how to go from 1-0, yes-no, to the solution of particular real-world tasks, using meaningful "language." Such program instructions are referred to as "software." The computer itself is "hardware."

3. *Control*
   They interpret the data. Control refers to the sequence of steps used to solve problems.

4. *Calculation*

    They process and solve problems; that is, they give answers. This is done through the computer's arithmetic and logic unit.

5. *Output*

    They give the results to you.[6]

Clearly, the computer's capacity to store information for future use is important. Thus an important question to be asked about any computer's capabilities is: How many bits or bytes can it hold in its memory *and* how many instructions can it put out per second?

While computer memory, like human memory, varies in capacity, computers, like humans, utilize both inside and outside resources as storage facilities. Humans have access to such storage devices as brains and libraries of books; computers have access to such storage devices as memory chips, disks, tapes, and cassettes.

Finally, another crucial question that must be asked also pertains to computer capability. While switches can be opened and closed at utterly thrilling speeds, they must do so in a sensible way or they will produce incoherent and bizarre output. So, the question must be: how good is this computer's "software"? That is, how good is the program which gives the specific instructions dedicated to having this computer interpret, process, and solve? Does it do the job sensibly and productively? As speed and storage capacity increase apace, programming problems become more complex, and the results are not always sensible. It could be argued that in some instances software goofs are actually getting out of hand.[7]

There are other serious computer problems on the horizon for experts to ponder, including, but hardly limited to, the issue of contamination: for example, the security of computer information with regard to both theft and "virus" infection. There is also the issue of the limits of miniaturization. At chip sizes below one micron (one millionth of a meter), circuit parts can go haywire because they don't have enough atoms left in them to assure stable functioning.[8] Moreover, the basic structure (architecture) of current computers—even supercomputers operating at ten billion cycles per second—is such that they may be approaching their fundamental physical limits. That is, they may be on the verge of obsolescence in the face of an ever-growing demand for newer and faster applications.[9] Finally, who will create and maintain the software for fabulous new bursts of computer power? For example, for parallel computer architecture (which operates through the use of several units working on different pieces of a problem at the same time). The new Cray supercomputer (the Y-MP model) uses eight processors to divide problems, solve the separate parts separately, and then verify the solutions. Other researchers are at work on sixty-four-parallel processor machines.[10]

Then, of course, there is the problem of memory capacity. Memory chips (called DRAMS and Static RAMS) must hold a lot of data for computer calculators to work on at, say 16 million calculations a second. As machines get faster and faster, memory capacity could become a problem.[11] Help may be on the way here. Erasable optic disks for personal computers are around the corner; that is, 5¼-inch disks that will hold 500 megabytes in your own little PC—enough for 250,000 typewritten pages.[12] Also, engineers at the University of California at Santa Barbara seem to be onto something "big" in energy conductors: webs of electronic wires so tiny (six million equal the width of one human hair) that they occupy only *two* dimensions, length and width. We are now into quantum structures![13]

CORPORATE

SOCIAL

RESPONSIBILITY

What Is It All About?

Corporate social responsibility is not merely the equivalent of corporate philanthropy. It is important that corporations with sufficient profit growth give money to public broadcasting efforts, to local symphony orchestras, to local substance abuse rehabilitation programs, and the like.[1] However, social responsibility has to have a broader meaning than is conveyed by mere dollars and cents.[2]

Ethical behavior is an integral part of the responsibility every corporation, like every individual, owes toward that society in which it exists and continuously interrelates in the process of taking and giving. Such behavior, such social responsibility, is independent of the size of this year's profit margin. Moreover, to the extent that any corporation abuses that responsibility, it abuses that society, and establishes its own personal threat, however small, to that society's continued healthy existence.

Philosophers, in and out of economists' garb, raise the issue of whether a body corporate can be thought of as having any moral responsibility at all. Others argue that even if corporations do have some sort of moral responsibility, it is no more than the equivalent of not breaking the prevailing law. Many more manifest their concern with the impossibility of drawing *any* substantive meaning from the terms "ethical behavior" and "social responsibility."

Undoubtedly, the subject of corporate ethics and overall corporate social responsibility is today on

America's front burner. The number of books on the subject alone is proof that concern about it sells.[3] Articles reprinted in anthologies carry titles such as "Can a Corporation Have a Conscience?" together with "Why Corporations Are Not Morally Responsible for Anything They Do."[4]

Can a corporation as an entity be held to ethical standards in society? Or is that impossible because a corporation is an inanimate thing incapable of having any measurable intent? It is difficult to conceive of an American public being concerned with the legal niceties of *actus non facit reum, nisi mens sit rea.*[5] The public has been far more likely to judge a corporation as a real entity, even to the point of characterizing collective corporate ethical and moral standards as at a lower level than those of people in the federal government.[6] What comes out of Widget Corporation is Widget Corporation's doing. When a Widget executive is sentenced to a prison term, that might be a personal tragedy or a law enforcement triumph or both, but one thing is surely clear: when the remaining executives and board members ask, after the felonious fact: "Now what do we do about our image?" they are referring to Widget's distinct, publicly determined persona as a *company.*

There is no denying that men run corporations (more than women as yet, for better or for worse) and that corporations cannot "act" apart from the people they are composed of. But there is also no denying that the people who make up corporations benefit enormously, and in many ways, from the corporation's distinct legal persona; moreover, it is only through the existence of that discrete persona that they are collectively able to affect the society as a whole, as well as individuals in it. There is no room in the public mind, nor should there be, for some rule of corporate ethical immunity, no matter what theoretical argument such a rule is grounded in, including a Kantian metaphysics of morals.[7]

Economist Milton Friedman has argued that a corporation's only social responsibility is to increase its profits while obeying the law and the rules of ethical custom.[8] *Ethical custom* is the joker in Friedman's deck, and he never makes its meaning clear. It would seem to mean a moral level of behavior beyond that required by law which could affect profit priorities. In sum, the conservative Nobel laureate would appear to have opened his own door a bit to the entrance of some social responsibility requirements for the corporation after all. Elsewhere, in the same article in which he refers to a need to follow the rules of ethical custom, Friedman seems to indicate that only existing law needs to be followed in such areas as corporate pollution of the environment.

The argument that adhering to the letter of the law satisfies social responsibility was confronted best by an admonition of Sir Thomas Browne some three hundred years ago: "Let not the law of thy country be the non ultra of thy honesty; nor think that always good enough which the law will make good."[9] More recently, a famous legal philosopher, H. L. A. Hart, wrote:

In all communities there is a partial overlap in content between legal and moral obligation. . . . Characteristically, moral obligation and duty, like many legal rules, concern what is to be done, or not be done, in circumstances constantly recurring in the life of the group. . . . The social morality of societies . . . always includes certain obligations and duties requiring the sacrifice of private inclination or interest which is essential to the survival of any society so long as men and the world in which they live retain some of their most familiar and obvious characteristics.[10]

There is little power in the argument that, as corporations or individuals, we benefit ourselves, our institutions, and our society as much as we can or ought so long as we simply do unto others within enforceable legal restrictions. One of the complications is that there are too many interrelationships affecting us all that do not have to do with the law. One of these is trust between people, better left to society and its institutions to sustain than for the law courts to put a price on.[11]

The simplest argument against the existence of corporate social responsibility—even if one concedes some sort of corporate persona—is that a corporation comprises its owners and their agents and nothing more, and therefore, whatever it does within the law is nobody else's business. This argument views the corporation as a private preserve, and the rest of us as poachers. If such *were* the case, it would be hard to see where corporate social responsibility *could* lie outside of that restricted relationship.[12] There are, however, at least two serious problems with this value-free, pseudo-scientific, economist's theoretical construct of the corporation.

First, these "self-contained" corporate entities make enormous use of the very society toward which they claim no responsibility (beyond not bending and twisting the existing law past the courtroom breaking point). For example, they use its tax-supported courts and legislatures to deal with their market failures and internecine warfare. Far more important, they function completely within an entire socioeconomic system of rights and obligations, of cultural values and beliefs, whose continued existence is the *only* guarantor of theirs. The idea that such a system can continue to support corporations in a healthy state without the corporate exercise of social responsibility toward *it* is surely problematical.

The proponents of this limited view of corporate existence and social responsibility claim, however, that the corporations in our economic system are, in fact, the protectors and guarantors of our political system. They argue that corporations provide the financial wherewithal that keeps our democratic way of life alive.

Herein lies the second serious problem. Our relatively free-market capitalist system has been and is the world's finest engine of economic growth; it has thus contributed to the support of our political system. But to argue that U.S. corporations have created, or continue to create, the conditions for liberty and equality is to misread the Declaration of Independence, the Constitution, the Bill of Rights, and our nation's history since 1776, at least.[13] The notion that corporate power and production are democracy's basic protectors, our bulwark against totalitarianism, misses the major point about the limits of every system of production. A renowned economist who was a determined free marketer and anti-collectivist put it this way more than thirty years ago:

It is by no means enough to invoke the laws of the market in appealing to people's enlightened self-interest and their economic reason . . . [since these often lead to attempts] to get more than genuine and fair competition would give. . . . There must be higher ethical values which we can invoke successfully: justice, public spirit, kindness, and good will . . . [and] respect for human dignity. . . . These . . . have to come from outside the market and no textbook in economics can replace them. . . . These are the indispensable supports which preserve the market and competition from degeneration.[14]

These indispensable supports, not material goods, must be the very basis of democracy's victory over totalitarianism.

Totalitarianism gains ground exactly to the extent that . . . human[s] suffer from frustration and non-fulfillment of their lives as a whole because they have lost the true, pre-eminently non-material conditions of human happiness. For this reason, it is certain that the decisive battle between Communism and the free world will have to be fought, not so much on the field of material living conditions, where the victory of the West would be beyond doubt, but on the field of spiritual and moral values. Communism prospers more on empty souls than on empty standards. The free world will prevail only if it succeeds in filling the emptiness of its own soul in its own manner and with its own values, but not with electric razors. . . . The material prosperity of the masses is not an absolute standard and a warning against regarding it as the West's principal weapon in the cold war is . . . justified.[15]

Every corporation is morally accountable to the society from which it extracts the essentials of its continued existence. And the term "corporate social responsibility" is one expression of that overall accountability.[16] A more difficult question asks what the exact parameters of that social responsibility might be. Certainly, corporate social responsibility is something more than giving away company money, and something less than a requirement to sacrifice corporate economic viability for the purpose of righting general societal wrongs. Beyond that, like so many other crucial social and ethical issues of our time related to power, wealth, economic growth, and the proper, positive roles of men, women, and institutions in society, there is no escape from the need to draw these parameters by means of individual judgments made in individual circumstances. The task is never easy, and we cannot afford to shirk it for some easy, faulty answers.[17]

NOTES

INTRODUCTION

1. The space footage and dollar figures on the PCC were taken from Bell of Pennsylvania's *Employee Information Booklet: Philadelphia Computer Center* (1986), p. 2. The material on the construction of the building is taken from Bell of Pennsylvania's *Philadelphia Computer Center, Fundamental Plan* (May 26, 1985) and from personal interviews with Ed Parsons, Philadelphia Computer Center Plan Manager, May 22 and June 3, 1987.

2. The information on pp. 4–8 is based upon the contents of the *Philadelphia Computer Center, Fundamental Plan*; *Glossary to Corporate Computer Center IV Facilities Study* (Bell of Pennsylvania, August 24, 1984); *Bell Telephone Company of Pennsylvania Annual Reports*, 1986 and 1987; and the following interviews: Ed Parsons, note 1,

above; Rich Masters, District Manager for Computer Operations and PCC head, Bell of Pennsylvania, May 13 and 29, 1987, and February 1, 1988.

3. CYBER is the vendor name of the Control Data Corporation Computer the PCC uses to perform this time-sharing function.

4. These figures are taken from *Bell Telephone Company of Pennsylvania Annual Report*, 1987, p. 9.

5. Interview with Ed Parsons, June 3, 1987.

6. Neal R. Peirce, Keynote Speech to the Pennsylvania Economic League 50th Anniversary Dinner, Philadelphia, Pennsylvania, November 19, 1986.

CHAPTER 1

1. Whether or not the dismemberment of AT&T was, in

fact, in the public interest is a subject for a separate book. An illuminating one is: S. Coll, *The Breakup of AT&T* (Atheneum, 1986), wherein the author argues that the public really lost by this particular government intervention.

2. *United States v. Western Electric and AT&T*, CCH Trade Cases (1982), paragraph 64,900.

3. *Bell Atlantic 1987 Annual Report*, p. 1.

4. John Brooks, *Telephone* (Harper & Row, 1976), pp. 20 and 341. *Telephone* is a thorough, fascinating, non-technical history of the telephone's first one hundred years, and of the Bell System as a whole. It points out that despite a tight-rein policy, when a subsidiary's earnings rose, Ma Bell's grip naturally loosened up a little; see p. 340.

5. *Plan for Computing and Information Systems in Support of the Mission of Temple University* (January 1984), chapter 5, "Goals and Objectives," pp. 38, 39 (my emphasis).

6. Philadelphians reduce that rather oddly spelled word to its essentials by pronouncing it "Skook'll."

7. Brooks, *Telephone*, p. 333.

8. Ibid., p. 336.

9. Interview with Carl Kleckner, Bell of Pennsylvania's ISO chief, May 21, 1987. The word "electronic" seems to confuse some people and it shouldn't. According to J. R. Pierce, the word "has come to mean all electrical devices for communications, information processing, and control" ("Electronics, Past, Present, and Future," *Science* 195 [1977]: 192).

10. Described in the Introduction, p. 7.

11. The multiple window example of impatience is from my interview with Ed Parsons, PCC Plan Manager, June 3, 1987. Parsons is not responsible for my overall conclusions regarding ISOs in telephone company families.

12. See my description of multiplex lines on p. 8.

13. Interview with Carl Kleckner, May 21, 1987. At the time, the issue of raising the western, Pittsburgh center to the level of the PCC was uppermost in Carl Kleckner's mind. His priority for the west, in my personal opinion, was not shared by all of his administrative superiors.

14. This reference is to Bell of Pennsylvania data centers only. Pennsylvania has never been a one-telephone-company state. While Bell of Pennsylvania is the major phone company for Pennsylvanians and Delawareans, it is not the only one. Actually, Philadelphia itself did not become a one-telephone-company town until 1945. Brooks, *Telephone*, p. 160.

15. Interview with Raymond W. Smith, former President and Chief Executive Officer of Bell of Pennsylvania, now President and Chief Executive Officer of Bell Atlantic Corporation, June 29, 1987.

16. Interview with Raymond W. Smith, June 29, 1987.

17. Liacouras holds degrees from Drexel (B.S.), the University of Pennsylvania (J.D.), the Fletcher School of Law and Diplomacy at Tufts (M.A.), and Harvard (LL.M); he has also been a temporary student at William and Mary and a Sterling Fellow at Yale.

18. *Inaugural Address Delivered by Peter J. Liacouras, October 28, 1982, in the Academy of Music*, Appendix III in *The Academic Plan for Temple University, Approved by the Board of Trustees*, May 13, 1986, pp. 55–57. Liacouras finished his formal address by referring to a letter of recommendation from one John Duff, headmaster of the only school his father had ever attended. His father proudly referred to that letter all his life as his "diploma." The letter read: "The bearer—James Liacouras—was a boy in St. Joseph's House some time ago. A good boy, a very industrious boy, one who could be relied upon. I have since heard nothing to make me change the above opinion of him. [Signed:] John Duff." Said son Peter, ending his inaugural address: "Some day, my friends, I hope the same can be said about me."

19. Interview with Peter Liacouras, President of Temple University, August 11, 1987.

20. Ibid.

21. Liacouras, *Inaugural Address*, p. 55.

22. Two documents that provide a good deal of insight into Liacouras's goals for Temple are his *Inaugural Address*, already cited; and his October 8, 1984, "Confidential Memorandum of October 2, 1984, Meeting with the Mayor of Philadelphia," reprinted in *The Academic Plan for Temple University, Approved by the Board of Trustees*, May 13, 1986.

23. These figures are extrapolated from *The Academic Plan for Temple University*, p. 68.

24. Ibid., pp. 59–60.

25. Ibid., p. 6.

26. Interview with James Hilty, Executive Officer of the President of Temple University, assisting the Vice President for Planning, Operations, and Health Services, June 11, 1987. Bill Cosby, by the way, is a member of Temple's Board of Trustees.

27. The report referred to is the *Plan for Computing and Information Systems . . .* , cited at note 5, above.

28. Interview with Robert G. Scanlon, Acting Vice President of Temple University, June 12, 1987; and interview with James Hilty, June 11, 1987.

29. Introduced by AT&T in 1961, Centrex allows the individual business customer to have its own switching exchange, with reduced-digit direct dialing among all of the sites in the exchange. Now such systems are often driven by powerful computers and offer extraordinary software-controlled, self-programmable features beyond the basic Centrex services described.

30. Interview with Bruce Gordon, Vice President for Sales, Bell of Pennsylvania, July 24, 1987; and interview with Robert G. Scanlon, June 12, 1987.

31. Ibid.

32. After divestiture, AT&T was no longer affiliated with locally operating telephone services.

33. Interview with James Hilty, June 11, 1987.

34. Interview with Bruce Gordon, July 24, 1987.

35. Gordon was on leave from Bell of Pennsylvania in 1987 as a Sloan Fellow at M.I.T.

36. Most of the following textual material relating to Ma Bell's history of social consciousness is derived from John Brooks, *Telephone*.

37. Quoted in Brooks, *Telephone*, p. 131.

38. Ibid., p. 132.

39. Ibid., p. 144.

40. Ibid., pp. 172–73.

41. Ibid., p. 205.

42. Ibid., p. 260.

43. Ibid., p. 285. It was during Romnes's period in office, in 1970, that the Equal Employment Opportunity Commission accused AT&T of discriminatory practices against racial minorities and women. In fact, AT&T had for several years been hard at work setting up a variety of programs for the hard-core unemployed in several U.S. cities and had publicly proclaimed its responsibility for participating in the social development of urban life. By the end of 1970, when the EEOC went after them, minority employees in the Bell System came to the same percentage as existed in the nation's population. It was not enough, and women at Bell, like most women in industry everywhere in the U.S. in 1970, *were* discriminated against. Romnes's beef was not in being told that there was more to do, but in being set up as *the* national non-doer villain. See Brooks, *Telephone*, pp. 287–88.

44. Ibid., p. 248.

45. Ibid., p. 250.

46. Ibid.

47. Andrew Heiskell, "Foreword," in *Teaching and Beyond: Nonacademic Career Programs for Ph.D.'s*, Teaching and Beyond Project (Regents of the University of the State of New York, October 1984), p. iv.

48. Interview with Gilbert Wetzel, President and Chief Executive Officer, Bell of Pennsylvania, June 10, 1987.

49. Interview with Bruce Gordon, July 24, 1987.

50. Interview with James Hilty, June 11, 1987.

51. Interview with James Mackin, Bell of Pennsylvania Division Manager for Real Estate, May 13, 1987.

52. Ibid.

53. Interview with Bruce Gordon, July 24, 1987.

54. Interview with James Hilty, June 11, 1987.

55. Interview with Raymond W. Smith, June 29, 1987.

56. Interview with Peter Liacouras, August 11, 1987.

57. Scanlon memorandum to Craig Shelter and David Brenner, then the Directors of the Philadelphia Industrial Corporation and the City Commerce Departments, respectively, August 31, 1984.

58. All the data in this paragraph are taken from *Draft North Philadelphia Plan* (Philadelphia City Planning Commission, October 1986), pp. 15–59.

59. Ibid., p. 41.

60. Ibid., p. 135.

61. It is estimated that the illiteracy rate in North Philadelphia for all those eighteen years of age and over is forty percent. Ibid., p. 135.

62. The data in this paragraph are from the *North Phila-delphia Databook* (Philadelphia City Planning Commission, 1986), pp. 9–23.

63. Some ten thousand structures in North Philadelphia are deserted—one-half of the total in all of Philadelphia. It is ironic that a sizable number of North Philadelphia's vacant lots are the result of demolition meant to get rid of public nuisances. See *Draft North Philadelphia Plan*, pp. 106 and 109.

64. L. B. Morrison, *The Community-Temple Charette* (Philadelphia City Planning Commission, 1970).

65. *North Philadelphia Databook*, p. 43.

66. Cf. *Academic Plan for Temple University*, pp. 4–6.

67. Liacouras, *Inaugural Address*, pp. 55–56.

68. Bell of Pennsylvania had, after all, failed in its bid to have Temple set up a Centrex system with Bell as the supplier. The Bell Atlantic–Temple contract, therefore, had been a loss for them. Any new relationship that brought some benefits to Bell would certainly have been welcomed.

69. Interview with Raymond W. Smith, June 19, 1987.

70. Liacouras, *Inaugural Address*, p. 57.

71. Interview with Raymond W. Smith, June 19, 1987.

72. Ibid. I am quoting Smith directly.

73. Ibid.

74. Ibid.

75. Interview with James Mackin, May 13, 1987.

76. Interview with Carl Kleckner, May 21, 1987.

77. Interview with Ed Parsons, May 22, 1987. See p. 9.

78. Interview with Harry Artz, North Philadelphia District Staff Manager Hardware/Software, ISO, May 21, 1987.

79. Interviews with Ed Parsons, May 22 and June 3, 1987.

80. "Bell of Pennsylvania North Philadelphia Urban Commitment." Two pages, with a drawing of the Temple Park area attached. Though undated, the textual material would seem to favor early August 1984 as the time of preparation of this document.

81. Ibid., p. 2.

82. *Draft North Philadelphia Plan*, p. 1.

83. The quote and all information in this paragraph are from Morrison, *The Community-Temple Charette*, pp. 65–66.

84. Ibid., p. 66.

85. Ibid.

86. *The Community-Temple Agreement of 1970* is a sixteen-page document, with the final page being the February 6, 1970, signatory page. My copy has a two-page "Summary Statement" (dated April 24, 1970) attached, as well as three maps and diagrams. The term "Charette" actually refers to the negotiating process through which the *Agreement* was reached; however, the word has come to encompass both process and product.

87. Morrison, *The Community-Temple Charette*, p. 77.

88. Interview with John Gamba, Vice President for Information Systems Operations (ISO), Bell Atlantic Corporation, Arlington, Virginia, June 4, 1987.

89. Interview with Raymond W. Smith, June 29, 1987.

90. Ibid.

91. Ibid.

92. The source for all materials pertaining to the Bell and Temple meeting on August 29, 1984, is a two-page memorandum to "Mr. Kelly and Mr. Smith" headed "Private," dated August 29, 1984, and signed by R. E. Young.

93. The two-page Bell "Project Planning Schedule" (draft, August 24, 1984), initialed by Mackin and Young, lists October 15 as the "go or no go decision between Temple site and Fort Washington 4-A site."

94. Schalch memo in Bell of Pennsylvania files, dated September 24, 1984. There is also a relevant memo from then Governor Thornburgh's Executive Director George Werner, to Bell (with accompanying letter) in the Bell files dated October 16, 1984.

95. This "confidential" memo was later reproduced in its entirety in a public document, *The Academic Plan for Temple University*, as Appendix IV. By 1986, dissident community groups had obtained all of this material on their own.

96. Robert G. Scanlon memo to Craig Shelter and David Brenner, August 31, 1984.

97. The memorandum to Smith from which the quoted material comes is signed by R. E. Young, and concurred in by the Vice President for Operations and Information Sys-

tem Organization, C. Hyde Tucker. There is one attachment, dated October 10, 1984, which is a map of the general Temple area, pinpointing the proposed site.

98. Bell files, memo dated October 23, 1984, signed by R. E. Young.

99. Two newspaper stories in 1984 emphasized the corroded condition of the SEPTA commuter train bridge beams in the area, and backed a relocation two blocks north to Berks Street; Philadelphia *Daily News*, November 23, 1984; and the Philadelphia *Inquirer*, November 25, 1984.

100. The figures are from the Philadelphia Industrial Development Corporation–Bell of Pennsylvania memo, dated November 5, 1984.

101. I was informed by Bell in April 1988 that "Congress has appropriated the money," and that "things are moving forward." At what rate of speed was not conveyed to me.

102. Schalch memo of December 19, 1984, Bell files, addressed to "Mr. Smith."

103. Schalch memo of December 27, 1984, Bell files, addressed to Smith.

104. "Urban renewal" and "inner city" are not, of course, synonymous. The outer areas of some cities have been rendered barren by industry shutdowns, for example. However, the reality is that our inner cities present the greatest problems in this area.

CHAPTER 2

1. Interview with Peter Liacouras, President of Temple University, August 11, 1987.

2. Ibid.

3. As far as I have been able to determine, a similar team, put to work to design a comparable computer center for the DuPont Corporation, required forty-five people.

4. Interview with Ed Parsons, PCC Plan Manager, May 22, 1987. While any errors made in this book in describing the structure and function of the Bell PCC are my own, most of the sensible articulation is the result of Ed Parsons's expert, patient explanation. Once he showed me the light, Rich Masters, District Manager for the PCC, was able, given his expertise, to make me understand what goes on in the

Center now; interviews with Rich Masters, May 29, 1987, and February 1, 1988.

5. *Philadelphia Computer Center Fundamental Plan*, Edward T. Parsons, Staff Manager, May 26, 1985 (hereinafter cited as PCCFP), pp. 9-1–4.

6. The main concern, of course, was that available space not be "exhausted." Computer Room Space Exhaust Forecast, PCCFP, p. 9-1.

7. Ibid., p. 6-3.

8. Interview with Ed Parsons, May 22, 1987.

9. There were, of course, PCC planning documents prepared prior to this one: the Building Planning Recommendation, October 15, 1984; the Building Specific Estimate #H2200, February 28, 1985; and an eleven-section *Corporate Computer Center IV* general overview information document, September 17, 1984.

10. The BOSS/BAC, SOP/DOE, COIN, and CYBER programs, described in the Introduction, pp. 6–8.

11. Interview with Ed Parsons, June 3, 1987.

12. Ibid.

13. "PCC Force Build-up," in *Marketing—Philadelphia Computer Center Visitation* (Bell of Pennsylvania, May 19, 1987).

14. Interview with Ed Parsons, June 3, 1987.

15. Ibid.

16. Interview with Larry Momarella, May 29, 1987.

17. Ibid.

18. Interview with James Mackin, May 13, 1987.

19. E. Colimore, "Thornburgh Signs Bills Funding Shelters, Police Training, and SEPTA," Philadelphia *Inquirer*, December 21, 1984.

20. Ibid.

21. P. Nussbaum, "SEPTA Looking for Outside Funds to Rebuild Station," Philadelphia *Inquirer*, January 17, 1985.

22. I refer primarily to my experience as Legal Counsel and Chief Executive Officer for the Office of the Coordinator of Addiction Programs, and as Commissioner of Addiction Services in the Human Resources Administration of the city of New York (1967–1970)—as well as my tenure as National Consultant for the drug education program of the United States Office of Education (1970–1980).

23. See statement of John A. Tuccillo, Chief Economist of the National Association of Realtors, quoted in M. L. Wald, "Managing Gentrification: A Challenge to the Cities," New York *Times*, September 13, 1987.

24. Wald, ibid.

25. L. W. Foderado, "Harlem's Hedge Against Gentrification," New York *Times*, August 8, 1987; A. DePalma, "Is the Upper East Side Moving North?" New York *Times*, January 31, 1988; J. Barry and J. Derivlany, *Yuppies Invade My House at Dinnertime* (Hoboken, N.J.: Big River Publishing, 1988).

26. M. Clements, reviewing *Yuppies Invade My House at Dinnertime*, in *New York Times Book Review*, April 17, 1988. Clements does not make that statement as a matter of personal belief, but as an observation on our "unfortunate refusal to deal with the gentrification phenomenon in a thoughtful, just, and imaginative way."

27. "America is moving backward—not forward—in its effort to achieve the full participation of minority citizens in the life and prosperity of the nation." *One Third of a Nation* (Commission on Minority Participation in Education and American Life, May 1988).

28. Liacouras, "Confidential Memorandum of October 2, 1984, Meeting with the Mayor of Philadelphia," in *The Academic Plan for Temple University . . .* (May 13, 1986), "Agenda Item 2," numbers 6 and 7.

29. Liacouras, *Inaugural Address*, in *The Academic Plan for Temple University* (May 13, 1986), p. 57.

30. Liacouras, "Confidential Memorandum," pp. 61–63.

31. Two interesting examples of healthy, constructive approaches to dealing with the gentrification problem can be found in the publication *Task Force Reports on Public Education, Youth Employment, and Housing, The Urban Affairs Partnership, 1985–86 Focus* (Urban Affairs Partnership, July 5, 1984); and in the actual work of *The National Temple Non-Profit Corporation* (NTNP), a fully staffed organization in North Philadelphia with a true community-based ethic stressing local participation in, and benefit from, the creation of affordable housing and the development of local commercial enterprise. It is church-based and not connected to Temple University. A fine example of non-gentrification neighborhood rehabilitation in Savannah, Georgia, is detailed in C. Warner, "Lee Adler Finds a Way," *Historic Preservation*, May/June 1988. On the issue of tenant management success, see I. Wilkerson, "From Squalor to Showcase: How a Group of Tenants Won Out," New York *Times*, June 11, 1988.

32. Interview with Paula Brown Taylor, Executive Director, East of Broad Community Development Corporation, December 1, 1988.

33. Ibid.

34. Philadelphia *New Observer*, March 14, 1985.

35. "North Philadelphia Hi-Tech Center Dropped," Philadelphia *New Observer*, July 3, 1985.

36. Interview with Raymond W. Smith, June 29, 1987.

37. Interview with Gilbert Wetzel, June 10, 1987.

38. Ibid.

39. Interview with Patrick Swygert, Temple Vice President for University Administration, June 26, 1987.

40. T. A. Frasca, "Some Don't Want Bell in N. Philly," *Temple University News*, April 2, 1985.

41. "North Philadelphia Hi-Tech Center Dropped," Philadelphia *New Observer*, July 3, 1985.

42. T. A. Frasca, ibid.

43. Interview with Charles A. Powell, District Manager, External Affairs, Bell of Pennsylvania, August 13, 1987.

44. Henry DeBernardo, quoted by Frasca, "Some Don't Want Bell . . ." *Temple University News*, April 2, 1985.

45. All fliers quoted from are in my files.

46. Flier in my files.

47. Interview with Charles A. Powell, August 13, 1987.

48. Data appear in *The Academic Plan for Temple University*, May 13, 1986, at pp. 65–67. See also *Temple University Office of Community Relations Program Directory*, 1988.

49. See section 14-1107 (c) of *The Philadelphia Code*.

50. At a meeting on April 9, 1985, sponsored by the Urban Affairs Partnership, the Reverend Cooper, who was present with Temple's Tom Anderson, said that "a key person who must be involved in the [Bell/Temple] strategy is Councilman John Street." A suggestion was made that Mayor Goode be approached so that he could "pave the way for support by Councilman Street." (UAP *Memorandum*,

dated April 12, 1985, in my files.) It is incredible that at this late date, with the Planning Commission process almost complete, Street had not yet been contacted. If the answer to that is that it was felt that the process needed to be completed *before* Street could cause trouble, then that answer is demonstrably deficient.

51. Quoted by L. Loyd in "Street Delays Approval for Bell Center," Philadelphia *Inquirer*, July 3, 1985.

52. Henry DeBernardo, "Inner City Squeeze: Battleground at Broad and Susquehanna," Philadelphia *New Observer*, March 14, 1985.

53. All references and quotes are from the April 19, 1985, letter from Councilman John Street to "Peter Liacouras, President, Temple University."

54. Rodney D. Johnson, vice president for Financial Affairs, "Councilman Street's Questions on Bell Development," memorandum to President Liacouras, April 25, 1985.

55. John Street, letter to David Cohen, Chairman of the Philadelphia City Council Rules Committee, May 21, 1985.

56. John Street, letter to David Cohen, May 21, 1985.

57. Joseph E. Coleman, President of the Philadelphia City Council, letter to Graham Finney, Chairman of the Philadelphia City Planning Commission, May 31, 1985.

58. *The Urban Affairs Partnership, 1985–1986 Focus—A Challenge to Philadelphia's Business, Community, and Public Leaders,* 1984; *The Urban Affairs Partnership, 1985–1986 Focus—Task Force Reports on Public Education, Youth Employment, Housing,* 1984.

59. Edwin W. Jordon, executive vice president, Barclay White, Inc., letter to the Hon. W. Wilson Goode, May 20, 1985.

60. Interview with Charles F. Schalch, assistant vice president for External Affairs, Bell of Pennsylvania, April 22, 1987.

61. Interview with Gilbert Wetzel, June 10, 1987.

62. Ibid.

63. Ibid.

64. Philadelphia *New Observer*, July 3, 1985, p. 10.

65. Interview with Paula Brown Taylor, December 1, 1988.

66. Interview with Gilbert Wetzel, June 10, 1987.

67. "North Philadelphia Hi-Tech Center Dropped," Philadelphia *New Observer*, July 3, 1985.

68. According to DeBernardo, the community group "demanded that Bell pay a high price . . . dish out the bucks if [it] wanted North Philly . . ."; "Inner City Squeeze," Philadelphia *New Observer*, March 14, 1985.

69. Interview with Larry Momarella, May 29, 1987.

70. My knowledge of these meetings first came from my interview with Charles Schalch, April 22, 1987.

71. Interview with David Brenner, former Director of Commerce, City of Philadelphia (now Chairman, Philadelphia Hospitals and Higher Education Facility Authority), July 23, 1987.

72. "Bell of PA to Temple: School's Out," Philadelphia *Daily News*, June 28, 1985; "Street Delays Approval for Bell Center," Philadelphia *Inquirer*, July 3, 1985; "North Philadelphia Hi-Tech Center Dropped," Philadelphia *New Observer*, July 3, 1985.

73. Interview with David Brenner, July 23, 1987.

74. Interview with Carl Kleckner, May 21, 1987.

75. L. Loyd, "Street Delays Approval for Bell Center," Philadelphia *Inquirer*, July 3, 1985.

76. "North Philadelphia Hi-Tech Center Dropped," Philadelphia *New Observer*, July 3, 1985.

77. Pat Swygert of Temple was only one of several people I interviewed who credit Coleman with helping to force this PCC issue; interview with Patrick Swygert, June 26, 1987.

78. Interview with Mayor Wilson Goode, August 12, 1987.

79. Interview with Darryl Taylor, member of the Board of the East of Broad Community Development Corporation, July 21, 1987.

80. Interviews with Paula Brown [Taylor], Executive Director of the East of Broad Community Development Corporation, and Shirley Kitchen, elected Ward Leader and Chairwoman of the East of Broad CDC, July 28, 1987.

81. Interview with Paula Brown Taylor, December 1, 1988.

82. Interview with Gilbert Wetzel, June 10, 1987.

83. All the quotations are from G. A. Wetzel, "Corpo-

rate Citizenship: What Role Motive," *Corporate Monthly*, November 1986.

84. Interview with Ernest Jones, Executive Director, Philadelphia Urban Coalition, July 29, 1987.

85. "I endorse the idea of the Philadelphia Urban Coalition working with Bell of Pennsylvania on its proposed construction project in the Fifth Councilmanic District . . ."; John Street, letter to Gilbert Wetzel, August 28, 1985.

86. Interview with James A. Roundtree, Jr., Project Director, Philadelphia Urban Coalition, July 29, 1987.

87. Ibid.

88. Interview with Ernest Jones, July 29, 1987.

89. Interview with James A. Roundtree, Jr., July 29, 1987.

90. And of course it took both labor and contractor cooperation. Cf. Patrick B. Gillespie, Business Manager of the Philadelphia, Pennsylvania, Building and Construction Trades Council, letter to Edwin Jordon of Barclay White, Inc., November 15, 1985.

91. Cf. James R. Bodine, Managing Partner, the Urban Affairs Partnership, letter to Charles Schalch of Bell, August 13, 1985.

92. *Norris Homes Career Mobility Center*, booklet published by Center for Social Policy and Community Development, School for Social Administration, Temple University (1986), p. 1.

93. Interview with Seymour J. Rosenthal, Director, Temple University Center for Social Policy and Community Development, June 17, 1987.

94. NTNP is church-based and not connected with Temple University.

95. All textual material related to the four areas discussed, insofar as it relates to what was said and done at the two 1985 meetings, is taken from the following two sources: *Minutes of Meeting, October 2, 1985, ECC 18th Floor* (Bell of Pennsylvania files); and *Minutes of Temple Meeting, November 5, 1985* (Bell of Pennsylvania files), together with all attachments.

96. Attachment to *Minutes of Meeting, October 2, 1985*.

97. John Street, letter to Councilman David Cohen, May 21, 1985, p. 2.

98. *Minutes of Temple Meeting, November 5, 1985*, p. 2.

CHAPTER 3

1. All data come from Bell of Pennsylvania, *Temple Task Force Reports*; in this case, those of the meetings of March 18, April 29, June 5, and October 10, 1986.

2. Bell of Pennsylvania, *Temple Task Force Report*, meeting of January 14, 1986.

3. C. A. Powell, *Employment, Technical Assistance and Grant-In-Aid to North Central Philadelphia Organizations Within a Memorandum of Understanding by Bell of Pennsylvania* (Bell of Pennsylvania, June 25, 1987), p. 4. Hereinafter cited as *Aid to North Central Philadelphia*.

4. John Street, letter to Councilman David Cohen, May 21, 1985, par. 4.

5. Bell of Pennsylvania, *Temple Task Force Report*, meeting of January 14, 1986.

6. Interviews with Charles Ashley, Bell District Manager/Affirmative Action, and Lou Walls, his key aide responsible for equal opportunity compliance and for any new hiring at the PCC project, May 22, 1987.

7. N. Wiener, *The Human Use of Human Beings: Cybernetics and Society* (Houghton Mifflin, 1950), cited in D. Hanson, *The New Alchemists* (Little, Brown & Co., 1982), pp. 65–66, 331.

8. "Report on the Production and Accomplishments of Member Organizations for 1986" (Community Development Coalition, Inc., Philadelphia, 1987). For an up-to-date analysis of the structure and function of CDCs in the United States, see N. Pierce and C. Steinbach, "Corrective Capitalism: The Rise of America's Community Development Corporations," *Ford Foundation* (88 pp.), 1988.

9. Interview with Paula Brown Taylor, Executive Director, and Shirley Kitchen, Chairwoman, East of Broad Community Development Corporation, July 28, 1987.

10. Interview with Elaine Black, Deputy Director, Philadelphia Department of Commerce, December 1, 1988.

11. Interview with Elaine Black, July 16, 1987.

12. Interview with Ernest Jones, Executive Director, Philadelphia Urban Coalition, July 29, 1987.

13. Lee Valenti, NDC Executive Director, letter to Charles Powell, District Manager, Bell of Pennsylvania, December 16, 1985.

14. Flier in my files, dated March 21, 1986.

15. C. A. Powell, *Aid to North Central Philadelphia*, p. 8.

16. Data in this paragraph are from the report of the Board of Directors Annual Meeting of the Urban Affairs Partnership, December 4, 1985, p. 6.

17. Data taken from Seymour J. Rosenthal, letter to Patrick Swygert, January 6, 1987; with accompanying statement, "Norris Homes Career Mobility Center Activity Report, December, 1986" (referred to hereafter as "Norris Homes Activity Report").

18. This and all other Betty Jackson quotes come from my interview with Betty Jackson, Community Organizer for the Norris Homes, December 1, 1988.

19. "Norris Homes Activity Report"; *Aid to North Central Philadelphia*, p. 11.

20. "Norris Homes Activity Report."

21. Ibid.

22. "Cosby Scholarship Recipient Announced," Philadelphia *Inquirer*, June 27, 1986.

23. The brochure made clear some interesting East of Broad CDC "political" attitudes: Registration fees were $0 for residents, $5 for students, $10 for "non-residents and business persons" and $15 for "public officials."

24. Interview with James Hilty, June 11, 1987. Then Director of the New Haven park, Sam Chauncy, was most cooperative, even appearing in a videotape made by Chuck Powell of Bell, which I have viewed, in order to explain his operation.

25. Referred to hereafter as *Temple Science/Jobs Program*.

26. Interview with William Tash, Temple Vice-Provost for Research in Graduate Studies and Acting Dean of the Graduate Schools, June 12, 1987.

27. *Temple Science/Jobs Program*, pp. 5 and 17; and interview with William Tash, June 12, 1987.

28. Interview with William Tash, June 12, 1987. The new Dean of the Temple Law School, William C. Dankelburg, is a former chief economist for the National Federation of Independent Business and was named, in 1979,

as the Small Business Administration "Research Advocate of the Year." Says Tash: "He will have responsibility for helping small minority-owned businesses in North Philadelphia."

29. The quotations are from my interview with Bonnie Squires, June 17, 1987.

30. L. Loyd, "$1 Million Bell Check Endows Temple Chair," Philadelphia *Inquirer*, November 11, 1986. Lest it be thought that Temple is the sole Bell beneficiary in this regard, it should be pointed out that Penn State University also received a similar donation for a similar chair. Penn State is CEO Wetzel's alma mater. Lest it be thought that ratepayers pay for these chairs in the end, Wetzel is quoted, in the *Inquirer* story cited, as assuring the public that they do not: "This and other charitable contributions come from the stockholders. We do it as a corporation, and there is no support from the ratepayer."

31. Governor Robert P. Casey had been having second thoughts about attending. While completely convinced that Bell's North Philadelphia commitment was due the highest praise, he and Bell of Pennsylvania were in the midst of a public flap of sorts. Gil Wetzel, speaking at a seminar at the University of Pennsylvania in November 1986, had developed a concept related to state telephone regulation. Under this concept, all services rendered by the telephone company, except for Public Service Commission-regulated basic phone service, would be deregulated; i.e., Centrex, Wide Area Telephone Service (WATS), and the like would be left to market forces. In return, the telephone company would donate $20 million per year from these deregulated businesses to a Telecommunications Economic Development Partnership Fund dedicated to state economic development efforts. The concept was interesting, and open debate on it in the legislature may well have brought out the fact that Bell of Pennsylvania, the State of Pennsylvania, and the free market system could have gained much by such a move. Bell of Pennsylvania, however, chose to discuss the idea first directly with Casey (on April 1, 1987), presumably to see if he thought it would fly. That, of course, was an utterly foolish step. What might have been perceived as a bold, innovative idea (even if disagreed with) became instead, when news of the meeting was leaked, a "secret plan"

and an "attempted bribe," etc. When news of the meeting was leaked in mid-April before the legislature had a chance to debate it publicly, the result was newspaper headlines (for example, "Bell Shoots Self in Foot," the Harrisburg *Patriot*), and a public rejection of the plan by the governor and an eventual backing off by Bell. Here, as in North Philadelphia, Bell learned a lesson in how *not* to go about developing effective partnerships!

32. Councilman John Street was invited and listed on the program as a speaker, but he never came. Given the excellent relations prevailing between the community and Bell, one can only assume that his snub was meant for Peter Liacouras. Street had also held up a council vote on the variance required to build the PCC garage a few months earlier, but in the total scheme of things that fit of pique was really anticlimactic.

33. Editorial, Philadelphia *Tribune*, May 1, 1987.

34. Editorial, Philadelphia *Inquirer*, April 30, 1987.

35. The quotes are from my personal notes taken at the opening ceremonies.

CHAPTER 4

1. Interviews with Rich Masters, May 13 and 29, 1987, and Feburary 1, 1988.

2. Information from interview with Charles A. Powell, Bell of Pennsylvania, December 1, 1988.

3. Several of my Bell of Pennsylvania interviews confirmed this obvious reality.

4. For a fuller picture of PICs, and a broader look at the Jobs Training Partnership Act, see: *The Forgotten Half: Pathways to Success for America's Youth and Young Families, Final Report on Youth and America's Future* (Wm. T. Grant Foundation Commission on Work, Family, and Citizenship, November 1988), esp. Chapter 5, "Toward Better Jobs for the Forgotten Half." This outstanding report will be referred to hereinafter as *The Forgotten Half*.

5. The Philadelphia City Planning Commission released the final version of its *Guide* to the revitalization of North Philadelphia in April 1988. Although its numerical data are much the same as that contained in the earlier version cited in this book, it does contain up-to-date material on develop-ment in various neighborhoods, including a brief East of Broad section. As a text on existing conditions, issues, opportunities, goals, and strategies, it deserves high marks: *North Philadelphia Plan: A Guide To Revitalization* (1988).

6. Interview with Paula Brown Taylor, December 1, 1988.

7. Patrick Swygert, letter to Paula Brown Taylor, August 9, 1988.

8. Interview with Paula Brown Taylor, December 1, 1988. East of Broad CDC/private developer talks are also referred to in B. Demick, "Princes of the City—Where Some See Squalor, Developers See Opportunity," Philadelphia *Inquirer*, November 27, 1988.

9. Interview with Paula Brown Taylor and Shirley Kitchen, July 28, 1987.

10. Interview with Shirley Kitchen, July 28, 1987.

11. Joint interview with Charles Powell and Elaine Black, December 1, 1988.

12. All quotes are from my interview with Betty Jackson, December 1, 1988.

13. See. p. 40. For a general outline of Temple activity with schools and community people, see *Office of Community Relations Program Directory* (Temple University, 1988), pp. 18–21.

14. *North Philadelphia Plan: A Guide to Revitalization* (April 1988), p. 78.

15. See p. 29.

16. R. E. Heckert, "Competitiveness and the Quality of the American Workforce." Testimony before the Subcommittee on Education and Health of the Joint Economic Committee, U.S. Congress, Washington, D.C., December 3, 1987. Quoted in *The Forgotten Half*, p. 93.

17. *Children in Need: Investment Strategies for the Educationally Disadvantaged* (Committee for Economic Development, New York, 1987), p. 3, cites "nearly 1 million." This publication will be referred to hereafter as *Children in Need*. Another publication, *A Call for Action to Make Our Nation Safe for Children: A Briefing Book on the Status of American Children in 1988* (Children's Defense Fund, 1988) in Part 1 uses the figure 750,000. This work will be referred to hereafter as *A Call for Action*. David D. Kearns, Chairman of the Board of Xerox Corporation, cites a figure

of 700,000 dropouts each year: Kearns, "An Education Recovery Plan for America," *Phi Delta Kappan*, vol. 69, no. 8 (April 1988): p. 566.

18. *Children in Need*, p. 3.

19. Ibid.

20. J. C. Simpson, "A Shallow Labor Pool Spurs Business to Act to Bolster Education," *Wall Street Journal*, September 28, 1987.

21. *A Call for Action*, Part 1, "Elementary and Secondary Education," p. 8.

22. The figure given in *A Call for Action* is 100,000 white dropouts per year.

23. Ibid.

24. *The Forgotten Half*, p. 26.

25. See pp. 29.

26. F. G. Diaz, "Mexico's Path from Stability to Inflation," in *World Economic Growth*, A. C. Harberger, ed. (Institute for Contemporary Studies, 1984) p. 365–66.

27. J. C. Simpson, "A Shallow Labor Pool . . . ," *Wall Street Journal*, September 28, 1987.

28. Quoted by Simpson, ibid.

29. "Back to the Basics," *Newsweek*, September 21, 1987, pp. 54–55. Other comments on this subject: "It's not . . . reading, writing, arithmetic now; it's new interpersonal skills, teamwork skills, logic skills, the ability to learn, problem solving skills, critical thinking skills . . . education is the weak underbelly of American competitiveness" (G. Melloan, "Public Education's Failures Plague Employers," *Wall Street Journal* [June 21, 1988]); "The New York Telephone Company . . . last year tested 60,000 applicants before it found 3,000 qualified to be operators. Basic skills include being able to speak the English language, file names in alphabetical order, do simple math correctly and read instructions" (T. Lueck, "Pervasive Problems Threaten New York's Economic Base," New York *Times* [June 26, 1988]). See also: *Workforce 2000* (Hudson Institute, 1987) and *Projections 2000* (U.S. Department of Labor, Bureau of Labor Statistics, 1988); and J. R. Swinton, "Service-Sector Wages: The Importance of Education," in *Economic Commentary*, Federal Reserve Bank of Cleveland, December 15, 1988.

30. F. Levy, "Income Distribution, A Growing Gap Between Rich and Poor," New York *Times*, May 1, 1988.

America is not the only nation concerned about the problem of education and its future. In England, seventy-two senior business leaders in a recent national survey made clear their belief that poor education in the face of new critical skills needs was their nation's top-priority problem, ranking ahead of inflation, interest and exchange rates, and improving the infrastructure: "Industrialists' Views on Government Policy Priorities," *The Financial Times*, September 28, 1988.

31. Anthony Lewis calls attention to Professor Paul Kennedy's chilling historical comparisons of America now and Great Britain in the early 1900s, with regard to these issues, in "Facing the Problems," New York *Times*, November 13, 1988.

32. Editorial, Washington *Post*, July 25, 1988, cited in *The Forgotten Half*, p. 138.

33. Data from research staff of the American Council on Education, summarized in Democratic Leadership Council, "National Service Fact Sheet," 1988; cited in *The Forgotten Half*, pp. 132, 168. See also L. A. Daniels, "Ranks of Black Men Shrink on U.S. Campuses," New York *Times*, February 5, 1989.

34. National Research Council, cited in the *Wall Street Journal*, March 1, 1988.

35. "Table 1A, Number of Doctorate Recipients by Citizenship, Racial/Ethnic Group and Subfield, 1986," National Research Council, Office of Scientific and Engineering Personnel, Doctorate Records File, 1988. Hereinafter referred to as *NRC Doctorate Records File*.

36. Cited in C. Sims, "Engineering in a Slump," New York *Times*, October 11, 1987.

37. Coined by the Advertising Council's Volunteer Advertising Agency, Young and Rubicam, Inc. See: *Moving America to Action*, The Advertising Council Inc. 1987–1988 Annual Report, p. 10.

38. *NRC Doctorate Records File*. See also M. I. Sovern, "Higher Education: The Real Crisis," *New York Times Magazine*, January 22, 1989, esp. at p. 56 on the Federal Graduate and Professional Opportunity Program.

39. I know of no group more knowledgeable, more vocal, and more responsible in the area of the problems of children of any age than the Children's Defense Fund in

Washington, D.C., led by Marion Wright Edelman. Nor is any recent publication in the area more important than the Children's Defense Fund's *A Call for Action*.

40. *Children in Need*, pp. x, 11, and Chapter Two ("The seeds of failure are planted early . . .").

41. Cf. M. Novak, "Top and Bottom: Who's Who?" *Wall Street Journal*, May 24, 1988.

42. C. P. Wharton, Jr., "Public Education and Black Americans: Today's Crisis, Tomorrow's Disaster?" Plenary Address to National Urban League Conference, San Francisco, July 21, 1986, pp. 6, 10.

43. Both programs are outlined in *The Forgotten Half*, pp. 121, 169.

44. The Boston Compact is described in *The Forgotten Half* at Appendix D, and in *Children in Need*, pp. 71–73.

45. The California Compact is described in *The Forgotten Half* at Appendix D.

46. The Cleveland Initiative is described in *The Forgotten Half* at Appendix D.

47. "An Education in Cleveland Now Comes with Something Extra: A Future," *Wall Street Journal*, May 26, 1988 (advertisement).

48. See *The Forgotten Half*, p. 192.

49. The Comer Process is discussed in *Children in Need*, p. 44; and in J. P. Comer, "The Social Factor," New York *Times*, August 7, 1988.

50. L. Thurow, *The Zero Sum Solution* (Simon & Schuster, 1985), p. 187.

APPENDIX 1

1. The general explanation of computers as switches is interestingly laid out in Fishman, *The Computer Establishment* (Harper & Row, 1981), pp. 7–11.

2. The miniaturization figures are contained in B. R. Schlender, "Intel's Development of 386 Computer Chip Took $800 Million and Four Years Difficult Work," *Wall Street Journal*, August 29, 1986. The same issue of the *Wall Street Journal* contains an article by R. L. Simison, "Thinking Small: New Computer Chips Promise More Power in Much Tinier Places," in which Simison contrasts computer chips, angels, and the heads of pins: ". . . today you can

line up about 1,000 transistors across the head of a pin and soon it will be 2,000." And if AT&T's Bell Labs can perfect its recently announced experimental tiny transistor, a mere 2,000 of them won't amount to much. The Bell Labs transistor is "too small to be seen even in the most powerful light microscope" (D. Stipp, "Bell Labs Expects Transistor to Improve Chips," *Wall Street Journal*, March 2, 1988). In fact, Bell Labs announced recently that its scientists successfully shrank semiconductor materials down to almost molecular size (J. Bishop, "Scientists Shrink Chip Materials to Atomic Size," *Wall Street Journal*, January 31, 1989). And Intel's new Reduced Instruction Set Computer (RISC) chip will hold *one million* transistors on a single fingernail-size sliver of silicon! (B. Schlender, "Intel Is Developing a New Type of Chip," *Wall Street Journal*, January 12, 1989).

3. Examples of such languages are COBOL (Common Business Oriented Language) and FORTRAN (Formula Translator Science/Math Language).

4. The *Britannica* illustration is extrapolated from data in "A Superconductor Dream Come True," *Newsweek*, October 12, 1987, p. 98. See also D. Stipp, "New Superconductor Research Indicates Communications Capabilities," *Wall Street Journal*, October 2, 1987.

5. A corporation named Sun Microsystems in California is presently working on a new "Space Station" or "Client Server" concept. Through this system, a new generation of powerful desktop personal computers linked to more powerful mainframe data bases and other large computers could have their instructional power increased up to the hundreds of millions of instructions-per-second range. See L. Kehoe, "Why Pundits See Sun a New Champ of the Valley," *Financial Times*, February 10, 1988. Additionally, another approach promising faster results is one utilizing Reduced Instruction Set Computer Chips (RISC) which allegedly work faster on less complex instructions. The Motorola RISC Chip 88000 allegedly performs 14–17 million instructions per second: L. Kehoe, "Why the Future of U.S. Chipmakers Is in RISC," *Financial Times*, April 26, 1988. The non-supercomputer mainframe market seems to have reached already the 100 million IPS level: J. P. Miller, "Amdahl Unveils a Faster Line of Computers," *Wall Street Journal*, May 4, 1988. Wang's newest *mini*computer appears to be capa-

ble of operating at 14 million IPS. W. Bulkely, "Wang Unveils Minicomputer at High End," *Wall Street Journal*, January 31, 1989.

6. The guide used for putting together the 5 functions material was Considine and Considine, eds., *Van Nostrand's Scientific Encyclopedia* (Van Nostrand Reinhold, 6th ed., 1983), p. 923. The entire entry "Digital Computer," pp. 922–28, is superb.

7. P. B. Carroll argues just that in "Computer Glitch—Patching up Software Occupies Programmers and Disables Systems," *Wall Street Journal*, January 22, 1988.

8. R. L. Simison, "Thinking Small: New Computer Chips Promise More Power in Much Tinier Places," *Wall Street Journal*, August 29, 1986.

9. G. Gilder, "One Man, One Cray," *Wall Street Journal*, August 26, 1987.

10. G. Melloan, "Staying Ahead of the Pack at Cray Research," *Wall Street Journal*, February 23, 1988.

11. P. H. Lewis, "Biding Your Time, in Nanoseconds," New York *Times*, May 1, 1988.

12. P. B. Carroll, "Devices Expected to Hasten Age of Optical Data Storage," *Wall Street Journal*, May 9, 1988.

13. P. B. Carroll, "Scientists Make Breakthrough in Effort to Build New Family of Electronic Parts," *Wall Street Journal*, January 30, 1989.

APPENDIX 2

1. United States corporations have done fairly well in this regard; corporate philanthropy has risen from $1.2 billion in 1971 to $4.5 billion in 1986. The last two years, however, seem to indicate a serious slowing down of growth in this area. See R. Stepneski, "Takeovers, Decline in Profits, Dampen Corporate Donations," *The Record* (Bergen County, New Jersey), February 21, 1988.

2. Equating corporate social responsibility with philanthropic dollars makes it easy to trivialize the entire social responsibility issue; it might seem that all that is really involved here is whether corporate giving to the local opera company is a product of the CEO's wife's entertainment preferences. Cf. T. Boone Pickens, quoted in the "Verbatim" section of the *Wall Street Journal*, July 19, 1987.

3. An abbreviated list would include: Cavanaugh and McGovern, *Ethical Dilemmas in the Modern Corporation* (Prentice-Hall, 1988); T. Tuleja, *Beyond the Bottom Line* (Facts on File, 1985); C. S. McCoy, *Management of Values: The Ethical Difference in Corporate Policy and Performance* (Pitman, 1985); Farmer and Hogue, *Corporate Social Responsibility* (Lexington Books, 2nd ed., 1985).

4. R. T. DeGeorge, "Can Corporations Have Moral Responsibility?" *University of Dayton Review* 5 (Winter 1981–1982); K. Goodpaster and J. B. Matthews, "Can a Corporation Have a Conscience?" *Harvard Business Review*, January/February 1982; M. G. Velasquez, "Why Corporations Are Not Morally Responsible for Anything They Do," *Business and Professional Ethics Journal* 2 (Spring 1983). All these articles are reprinted in Chapter 2 of Beauchamp and Bowie, eds., *Ethical Theory and Business* (Prentice-Hall, 3rd ed., 1988).

5. "An act does not make one guilty, unless one is so in intention."

6. A. Clymer, "How Americans Rate Big Business," *New York Times Magazine*, June 8, 1986.

7. Anyone who truly believes that a corporation has no substantial identity of its own has never been a buyer forced to kick the corporation's "good will" rock at the time of signing the contract of sale.

8. Milton Friedman, "The Social Responsibility of Business Is to Increase Its Profits," *New York Times Magazine*, September 13, 1970.

9. Sir Thomas Browne, *Christian Morals*, I.ii (published posthumously in 1716).

10. H. L. A. Hart, *The Concept of Law* (Oxford: Oxford University Press, 1961), pp. 166–67.

11. *Trust*, despite being what economists would call "an externality," has a "very important pragmatic value if nothing else. . . . [It] is an important lubricant of a social system." This is true even if, absent a legally imposed fiduciary duty, one can't sue because one's trust was corporately breached; K. Arrow, *The Limits of Organization* (Norton, 1917), at pp. 22–23. *Loyalty* is a concept much the same. Individual human and corporate teamwork and productivity is surely undermined when bonds of loyalty are destroyed and replaced with anger and resentment over dis-

loyal actions—even if no recovery for them is available in a court of law. See also A. Shleifer and L. Summers, *Breach of Trust for Hostile Takeovers* (NBER Working Paper Series no. 2342, National Bureau of Economic Research, August 1987); and W. Norris, "Ethics of Organizational Transformation in Takeovers, Plant Closings, and Cooperative Ventures," Remarks, 7th National Conference on Business Ethics, Bentley College, October 15, 1987.

12. Former Supreme Court Justice Arthur Goldberg was stunned by this attitude as a member of the Advisory Committee on Tender Offers, set up in 1983 as the result of a Senate Banking Committee request. In his separate statement to the Committee Report, Goldberg commented on the total intracorporate tenor of the Report this way: "The Report of [this] Committee makes no significant reference to the public [as well as the corporate] interest. This arises from the misconception that only shareholders are involved and not the public at large . . . [and this] is inadequate. . . . The stock market crash which contributed to the Depression in the 1930's . . . is proof enough of the public interest involved [in securities transactions]." Fox and Fox, *Corporate Management Acquisitions*, V.4 (Matthew Bender & Company, 1985), Appendix IX, letter, pp. 122*ff.*

13. The constitutional issues involved in property rights, civil rights, and the social welfare demand more space than this book can give them. Some proponents of the narrow view of corporate responsibility insist that property rights are constitutionally sacrosanct, that they hold an exalted position in our constitutional jurisprudence equal to that of any other "human right." Cf. Jensen and Meckling, "Theory of the Firm: Managerial Behavior, Agency Costs and Ownership Structure," *Journal of Financial Economics* 3 (1976), cited in Jensen and Smith, eds., *The Modern Theory of Corporate Finance* (McGraw-Hill, 1984) p. 80 n. 6. Jensen and Meckling are simply wrong. Of course we Americans have property rights. But the ultimate "right" is to get a fair price for our property if the government decides to take it away for their own legitimate purposes. That's called "due process." The government has *no way* to deprive us of any right to religious freedom, or of our right not to have a state religion foisted on us. There is no "due process" by which such nonnegotiable human rights can ever be paid away. See also the last sentence of Justice Stone's famous dissent in *Morehead, Warden v. New York ex rel Tipaldo*, 298 U.S. 587 (1937), in which he was joined by Justices Brandeis and Cardozo.

14. W. Ropke, *A Humane Economy—The Social Framework of the Free Market* (University Press of America, 1986), pp. 124–25 (emphasis supplied). Originally published as *Jenseits von Angebot und Nachfrage*, 1958.

15. Ibid., p. 111.

16. For a rather unusual expression of concern about the need for enhanced corporate social responsibility on the part of the U.S. and Great Britain, see J. Lloyd, "U.S. and U.K. Appeal to the Corporate Conscience," and the editorial, "The Caring Corporation," both in *Financial Times*, May 4, 1988. A report distributed by the White House in 1988 details this concern: "Special Supplement: The British-American Conference on Private Sector Initiatives, London, England, May 2–4, 1988" (White House Office of Private Sector Initiatives, Washington, D.C., 1988).

17. A famous American economist has cast the general issue of "responsibility" in terms of the ever-present tension existing between our economic institutions on the one hand and our political and social institutions on the other. His extended discussion is well worth reading: A. M. Okun, *Equality and Efficiency—The Big Tradeoff* (The Brookings Institution, 1975).

INDEX